PREFACE

N ow it is common knowledge that John Rawls' book *A Theory of Justice* (1971) initiated influential normative discourses that during the last two decades have dramatically changed the scene both within ethics and political philosophy. Thus meta-theoretical and historical orientations in reseach have been forced to give room to discussions dealing with substantial and normative problems of our contemporary modernity. This intellectual process, which started in America and has passed through most European countries as well, has influenced both academies and the wider political public. One of its major consequences has been the increasing demand for, and consequently the raising profile of, philosopy in various social and political contexts.

The new situation has had positive effects on academic discourses themselves. Thus, in the contemporary debates on the foundations and limits of liberalism as well as possible alternatives to its different versions, the historical backgrounds have been studied more intensively than perhaps ever before, and also with new insights. Some of the defenders of liberalism as well as their communitarian critics have been able to adopt very much the same kind of position of a mediator between tradition and the actual situation, between academic contexts and wider publicity, as did many classics on modern ethical and political thought (e.g. Hobbes, Locke, Smith, Rousseau, Kant and Hegel) in their time. This means that, most likely, we are nowadays better prepared to confront these classics on those levels of intentions on which they themselves worked.

The new situation can be clearly seen in contemporary Hegel-research. True, our picture of Hegel has been changed considerable by the new critical edition of his works – though we still have to wait for the new edition of *Rechtsphilosophie* – and by excellent new translations. But our picture has also changed because of the important efforts to understand Hegel's problems as well as many of his solutions in the light of our present normative concerns. After all, we are Hegel's contemporaries in several respects. Thus, through our present optics we are better able to understand and learn from Hegel's attempts to steer his philosophy of right between two unattractive enemies: the conservative defenders of the German tradition and the liberals, whose thinking in his eyes was always far too abstract and formal. Although many of Hegel's metaphysical arguments are difficult to follow (let alone to accept) today, they seem to make possible a very interesting position between various forms of liberalism inspired by both Hobbes and Locke as well as Rousseau and Kant, and communitarianism inspired by Aristotle and Herder, among others. Many recent studies of Hegel evidence that we can still learn a lot from him when dealing with the ethical and political problems of our time.

The contemporary discussions between liberals and communitarians certainly provide one of the contexts in which many of the studies in the present book have been written and in which they may be read. The present collection, however, was not intended in the first place to relate Hegel's thought to those discussions. The texts collected here were originally read in a colloquim in Jyväskylä in May 1996. To the meeting we invited Finnish scholars working with Hegel's philosophy of right and Dr. Michael Quante from Münster. Hegel's *Grundlinien der Philosophie des Rechts* was the theme of the meeting not only because of our scholarly interests in Hegel's book, but also because the book had appeared in Finnish

Jussi Kotkavirta (ed.)

Right, Morality, Ethical Life

Studies in
G.W.F. Hegel's Philosophy of Right

SoPhi

Publications of Social and Political Sciences and Philosophy 12

University of Jyväskylä

SoPhi

Publications of Social and Political Sciences and Philosophy
University of Jyväskylä

SoPhi is a publication series at the Department of Social Sciences and Philosophy, University of Jyväskylä, Finland. SoPhi publishes studies on social policy, sociology, political science and philosophy. Texts are chosen for publication on the basis of expert review.

The editorial board includes Kaj Ilmonen (Professor of Sociology), Eeva Jokinen (Research Fellow in Social Policy), Jussi Kotkavirta (Assistant Professor of Philosophy), Eerik Lagerspetz (Professor of Philosophy), Marjatta Marin (Professor of Social Gerontology), Kari Palonen (Professor of Political Science), Tuija Parvikko (Assistant Professor of Political Science), and Juha Virkki (publications editor of SoPhi).

Correspondence should be sent to the Department of Social Sciences and Philosophy/SoPhi, University of Jyväskylä, P.O. Box 35, FIN-40351 Jyväskylä, Finland. Publications can be ordered from Kampus Kirja, Kauppakatu 9, FIN-40200 Jyväskylä, Finland (tel. +358-(0)14-603157, fax +358-(0)14-611143, e-mail kkirja@bibelot.jyu.fi).

ISBN 951-34-0930-9
ISSN 1238-8025

Printed at Jyväskylä University Printing House, Jyväskylä, 1997

Cover printed at ER-Paino

Cover design by Carita Hyvärinen

Contents

Preface 1

Markus Wahlberg:
Punishment as Ideal Reconciliation and Real Regeneration 5

Tuija Pulkkinen:
Morality in Hegel's Philosophy of Right 29

Michael Quante:
Personal Autonomy and the Structure of the Will   45

Jussi Kotkavirta:
Happiness and Welfare in Hegel's Philosophy of Right 75

Markku Mäki:
Modern Society in Rousseau and Hegel 93

Ossi Martikainen:
The Principle of the Subjectivity and
Sittlichkeit in Hegel's Philosophy of Right 105

Eerik Lagerspetz:
Hegel and Hobbes on the Sovereignty of the People 119

Hannu Sivenius:
Remarks on Schelling's
Criticism of the Hegelian Idea of the State 135

as the translation of Markus Wahlberg in 1994.[1] The colloquium was thus a celebration of this event, as is this collection.

The present contributions discuss various parts and themes of Hegel's *Elements of the Philosophy of Right* (*PR*). *Markus Wahlberg*, who teaches criminal law in Helsinki, studies the interpretation and criticism of Hegel's theory of punishment as put forward by an influental legal scholar in Finland, Karl Gustav Ehrström, at the end of the last century. *Tuija Pulkkinen*, who currently conducts women studies in Helsinki, proposes an interpretation of Hegel's position in respect of Kantian morality and also discusses the ideas of the most important Finnish Hegelian of all times, J.V. Snellman, who in his reading of Hegel's *PR* emphasizes strongly the themes in the chapter dealing with morality.

Michael Quante, who teaches philosophy in Münster as an assistant of Ludwig Siep, a prominent Hegel scholar, discusses various contemporary theories of personal autonomy, suggesting that Hegel's holistic approach contains several ideas still worth serious reflection when we consider the principal problems of our contemporary theories. *Jussi Kotkavirta*, who teaches philosophy in Jyväskylä, discusses the notions of happiness and welfare as well as their roles in Hegel's argumentation, also indicating Hegel's significance for our contemporary discussions about the good life.

Markku Mäki, who teaches philosophy in Tampere, makes a broad comparison of Hegel's and Rousseau's ways of thinking about modern society, finding both interesting affinities and differences. *Ossi Martikainen*, who is a postgraduate student in Jyväskylä, discusses Hegel's paragraph 260, where the principle of subjectivity, according to Hegel a central aspect of modernity, is presented, indicating the roles this principle has in the theory of *Sittlichkeit* set out in *PR*.

Eerik Lagerspetz, who works as professor of philosophy in Jy-

---

[1] G.W.F. Hegel, *Oikeusfilosofian pääpiirteet eli luonnonoikeuden ja valtiotieteen perusteet*. Johdannon laatineet Juha Manninen ja Markus Wahlberg. Pohjoinen, Oulu 1994.

väskylä, discusses Hegel's and Hobbes' theories of constitution, comparing their arguments against the principle of the sovereignty of the people and placing Hegel in a broader context of constitutional development. Finally, *Hannu Sivenius*, who teaches philosophy in Helsinki, discusses F.W.J. Schelling's less known ideas concerning the state and his criticism of Hegel's *PR* after Hegel's death.

Jussi Kotkavirta

Markus Wahlberg

PUNISHMENT AS IDEAL RECONCILIATION AND REAL REGENERATION

Karl Gustaf Ehrström's Interpretation and Criticism of Hegel's Theory of Punishment[1]

Reconstruction and criticism of Hegel's views on punishment – one of his "favorite subjects"[2] – would of course require detailed historical and systematical study of the development and results of his absolute idealism. On the other hand: in the latest monographs[3] which concentrate on the subject especially in the context of the *Elements of the Philosophy of Right* (*PR*) there is a tendency to almost completely ignore what the Hegelian specialists in criminal law in the nineteenth century have accomplished. Karl Gustaf Ehrström's paraphrase and criticism of Hegel's theory of punishment as it is construed basically in the First Part of the *PR* will allow me to explicate my own position as a critic of a critical criticism in taking into consideration some other crucial passages from Hegel's treatise. For reasons that are easy to understand, I must abstract in this essay from Ehrström's own 'moving principle of the concept'[4] as he develops it as a critique of all the traditional relative and absolute theories of punishment in his various texts.[5] But I hope that the citations from PR will in a way compensate for Ehrström's purely "negative dialectic" by giving it a somewhat more concrete context.

Hegel, with his view on punishment as "the negation of the negation" and "the right of the criminal", is widely known. But who was Karl Gustaf Ehrström?

Karl Gustaf Ehrström (17 March 1822–23 October 1886) was a Finnish Hegelian and the most important draftsman of the total reform of the Finnish Criminal Law in the second half of the nineteenth century. With two other well-educated experts on criminal law he prepared the committee report of 1875, which was the basis for all central reforms of criminal law and especially of the Finnish Penal Code of 1889. Moreover, for all practical purposes he single-handedly prepared the draft of the general part of this code, which contains the philosophically most interesting concepts of criminal law. When the Penal Code was enacted some three years after his death, many of his proposed provisions were wholly abandoned or partially changed because they were seen to be "too theoretical". However, one can say that in its entirety the Penal Code is at least as much his creation as it is that of his pupil and successor Jaakko Forsman, professor of criminal law and legal history at the University of Helsinki.

As professor Ehrström held the chair from 1860 until 1877, when he was appointed senator at the Department of Justice of the Finnish Senate. In the spring of 1886 he was notified to assume the office of the Attorney General, the highest authority of justice within the Grand Dutchy of Finland as a part of Russian Empire; however he was able to discharge the duties of his office for only some five months before he died unexpectedly in October 1886.

Ehrström's printed literary production is not large, but the nearly 5 000 manuscript pages of his lectures in criminal law, legal history and other branches of jurisprudence fill one with respect for his ability and profoundness. In short: Ehrström was the founder of modern Finnish criminal law and criminal jurisprudence in the second half of the nineteenth century.

In his Lectures on the General Part of the Criminal Law from the Spring Semester 1860 to the Spring Semester 1861, based on Berner, Ehrström says that the concept of punishment has to be first developed or defined accurately if one seeks general principles of criminal law that are "articulated by philosophical speculation". And these principles are included "according to the concept" into theories of punishment. During the second half of the eighteenth century the theories proceeded from an attempt to find "the purpose of punishment", but at the beginning of the nineteenth century the main interest was "in explicating what punishment is".[6]

As we see, Ehrström accepts and then, in developing his own view, comprehensively but critically adapts the main principles of various utilitarian or relative theories of punishment whose basic interest is in the future prevention of crimes: *ne peccetur*.[7] But as a Hegelian, Ehrström's answer to utilitarians on this general level of the question is that one must first try to define the state's subjective right for the use of punishment and secondly the objective principles which the state has to observe in the use of this subjective right in practice.[8]

The gist of retributive or absolute theories as juridical retribution, *quia peccatum est*, is juridically that one has the right to punish only on condition that the act fulfills the general preconditions of criminal liability and the definitional elements of an offence according to the principle of legality and the requirement of voluntary conduct.[9] Therefore Ehrström explains to the utilitarians: "[t]he state namely cannot use punishment in a way which would differ from its nature... just as a table should not be used for anything else than to serve as a table; surely it does not occur to anyone to use a table as a horse or as some other thing besides a table. How could the state then be justified to use punishment for something else than to punish". And after this, should we say, short analytical analysis long before modern analytical philosophy, Ehrström concludes: "Something rational cannot refer to anything else than to what it is in accordance with its concept. Therefore punishment cannot be something else, and the state as a rational institution cannot be legitimized to use punishment as something other than punishment. But this entails that also in the use of punishment one cannot apply any other principles besides those which emerge from its own essence. In another words, one has to use punishment so that the use of it remains what it is, namely punishment."[10]

To put the matter very simply: if we don't first try to define or at least characterize the question with some abstract determinations, it is very plausible that fruitless dispute will result from the effort to understand what the word 'punishment' means every time it is used. That is Ehrström's point in his critique of the traditional relative and absolute theories, and one can say that his own dialectical "development of the concept" in its entirety shows how utilitarians and retributivists miss the point to the extent that they are not talking about the justification of the same practices or that their arguments have different weight at the different levels of criminal justice practice.[11]

Ehrström indeed recognizes many central utilitarian aspects at the general legislative and particular applicative levels of the criminal justice system, and especially with respect to the carrying out of an individual punishment.[12] And he even emphasizes that disputes between the retributivists and the utilitarians have been inevitable and produced many good results. But the utilitarians see the state as an institution which exists only for citizens, to protect their private interests and to promote their welfare, which in turn means that they don't realize that the state finds its justification "through its own self and its own existence".[13] But as already stated, here it is not possible to present Ehrström's "dialectic of theories of punishment" in its totality. Therefore we shall make – through some critical assessments – a transition to Hegel's theory.

Transition to Hegel's Theory

Ehrström criticizes the utilitarians or advocates of relative theories for neglecting the concepts of crime and punishment. But neither does he accept the absolute theories of Immanuel Kant, Karl Salomo

Zachariae[14] and Hermann Wilhelm Eduard Henke[15].

In Ehrström's opinion, Kant as a political theorist was also not consistent in that he let the state have its justification in the social contract[16] and yet saw punishment as a requirement of reason. Because the goal, end or purpose of the state did not lie in the state itself but in the protection of its members, Kant should have held that the end of punishment also lay in that protection. However, according to Ehrström, he stepped beyond this utilitarian and contractarian point of view when he saw in punishment a retributive end in itself. Therefore, Kant's reasoning on this point was inconsistent.[17]

Zachariae likewise based his theory on a similar view. Crime was not directed against the right in and for itself but against the individual rights of citizens. And if he had been logical he should have seen punishment as a means of protecting those rights. But he tried to see in it something higher – a retribution required by reason or justice. The crime on the other hand was not in Zachariae's theory an attack against rational order or system of the world. And hence a deep abyss lies between his concepts of crime and punishment.[18]

In Henke's theory, this abyss was slightly adjusted. According to Henke, a crime affected not only the outward social order but infringed also on the reason within the right being in and for itself; and crime was based on the guilt of an offender itself, whereof his conscience bears witness.[19] Therefore he saw crime as an attack on the eternally valid rational or absolute system of the world, of which every human being has a more or less clear consciousness in his conscience. But he did not recognize that this system of the world is not only present in an individual's conscience but in outward social life too. According to Ehrström, this social life also has its constitution in the spiritual laws of reason, which are totally independent of contracts and interventions of individual citizens of a state. But Henke saw in crime only an attack against the rational consciousness in an individual's conscience, but not an attack against the valid order of outward social life. According to his theory, therefore, punishment was directed only against an attack which a criminal had caused to himself in his conscience and not also against the criminal's attack upon the actually rational system of society.[20]

It is particularly Henke's emphasis on the subjective side of crime and its negation or punishment as the only morally ideal regeneration that Ehrström criticizes as one-sided. And the remedy for that narrowness of subjective or formal morality he seeks in Hegel. But first – as he says in his lectures – he wants to recapitulate "for the Gentlemen" Hegel's conception of the state. And so would I also like to do in this article.[21]

Comments on Hegel's Theory of the State

As we have already noticed, in certain passages Ehrström is in social or ethical theory a Hegelian who uses Hegel's philosophical-technical terminology not only in his conceptual developments in criminal law theory but also at the metaphysical and ethical level. But the reason for commenting more comprehensively on certain essential points in Ehrström's paraphrase of Hegel is the fact that he thereafter criticizes Hegel for being objectively one-sided in his theory of punishment.

Ehrström first paraphrases the Hegelian conception of the essence of the state: it does not have its ground in a contract between its members but in the eternally valid laws of reason which would rule even if the members of a society decided to dissolve the state. For, according to and led by their own rational or reasonable essence, they would inevitably constitute a new state. Whether they wished it or not, the necessity of reason would in any case coerce them to live as members of a state.[22]

A thorough explication of this passage would require a separate study of its own. Here I only wish to point out that in Hegel himself 1) the sting of the critique is directed against all the main social contract theories, should we say, from Hobbes to Fichte, which see the *exeundum e statu naturae* in different kinds of imaginary contracts between the members of society. And that is for Hegel, and for Ehrström too, most objectionable on the grounds that the natural law tradition intends to found the state on relations of abstract right and in particular on property relations, which are the proper realm of civil society, the realm where individual needs are created, satisfied and fortified with an ever-growing set of social and artificial desires.[23] But 2) at the same time our speculative idealists of course make sarcastic objections to reactionary absolutism, which treats the state as the monarch's private property with an arbitrary administration of justice, etc.[24]

Most of the social contract theorists, with the possible exception of Hobbes, accepted the basis of what was later to be called the rule of law state. And the same goes also for Hegel, particularly in the Section The Adminstration of Justice in *PR*. Hegel even systematically emphasizes the significance of the rule of law as a protective principle in civil society in locating its basic institution, the court of law, not in the state proper but in civil society, where it functions as the mediating conceptual formation between the two extremes: on the one hand the system of needs or economics and on the other hand the police and corporations.

Similarly, Ehrström has a realistic vision of the chances of the pure "coercion of reason" in bourgeois civil society: "[b]ut it does not follow that the concrete legislation should always and everywhere be in accordance with the eternally right; on the contrary, many bad laws exist which contradict the laws of reason.[25] Concrete legislation namely depends on the view of law and justice of its legislators, and this is, as is well known, highly variable – it depends on the cultural stand of the legislators".[26]

As an absolute idealist it is easy for Ehrström to be optimistic anyway: "[b]ut the concrete legislation must after all advance in more and more explicit comprehension of the eternally right and strive to bring it into force in itself. All of world history also bears witness to this progress."[27]

Hegel's Theory of Punishment

The premise is then constructed in itself. But Ehrström's paraphrase of Hegel's theory of punishment nevertheless fills nearly five pages.

In developing the premise I must therefore limit myself to citing only the main points of Ehrström's text without commenting at length on it or without comparing it thoroughly with Hegel's original.

Ehrström indeed accepts also Hegel's determination of the concept of right, which he paraphrases as follows: "[t]he right constitutes itself in those eternal laws of reason on which the state is based and as they manifest themselves in outward social order. The right is... thus the outward existence of the eternal reason in the state, and as such it is beyond any particular legislation, even if it has to manifest itself in particular laws."[28]

When Ehrström then begins to describe Hegel's theory of punishment, he emphasizes that in principle it deals with those "eternal laws of reason" and not with concrete legislation.[29] And those laws of reason constitute "the essence of the right" so that "the general rational will gives itself an outward existence". But because "the outward existence of reason" is precisely "the outward rational social order, it comprehends and contains the rights of all and everybody". Hence "the right is the basic concept of the rights of all and everybody, in which reason has its outward existence".[30]

This description paraphrases Hegel's characterization of the abstract realisation of the concept of the general free will in itself and in the external rights. But if the will is so in principle or, abstractly taken, absolutely free, how can one coerce it – for evidently there must be at least some coercion in crime and in its negative correlate, punishment? At the most general level, Ehrström continues, "[r]eason or the general will in itself cannot be coerced; it is only in those outward rights that its coercion is possible."[31] And then Ehrström paraphrases Hegel's concept of crime as it is determined in the section "Wrong" in "Abstract Right":

> The rationality of an individual has its ground in the equivalence of his will with the eternal reason or general rational will. If an individual will now infringes on some of those rights into which the existence of the rightful or general rational will differentiates itself, the individual exerts force on the general will. At the same time, however, he contradicts the rational essence within him-

self and therefore shows himself to be irrational. The crime is coercion which an individual will directs to the right; an infringement of the outward existence of rationality. The coercion which the crime contains, or the infringement of right caused by it, thus contradicts the rational system of the world.[32]

Therefore, according to the philosopher's standpoint, "[t]he right as eternally rational has to bring itself into force against that irrationality. In this way the right manifests its sovereignty as the second coercion directed against the individual will, cancelling the first act of coercion and restoring the right."[33]

Ehrström has thus determined the crime and punishment from the philosopher's standpoint. But he continues his paraphrase of Hegel and says that the crime's cancellation or negation is even the end or the goal of the punishment: "[a]nd because the punishment is itself just this cancellation of the negation of the right, punishment is for that reason a rational end in itself without any other ends". And then Ehrström comes to the crucial point:

"But in cancelling the wrong it at the same time restores the right and is thus just, and as such it is just not only as a requirement of reason or the general will but also as a requirement of the offender's own reason. For as a rational being he also recognizes this requirement of reason that the irrational, the wrong, the crime must be cancelled and that reason must reign. The law he has infringed on is also the general law of reason he has acknowledged, and for that reason he has infringed also on his own law which contains the commandment of the right not only for others but also for himself. Therefore it includes his right too, and when he is punished there happens nothing but what he has accomplished through his irrational act or crime and what he as a rational essence recognizes as right. Thus the punishment is justified also for the offender himself; and when being punished in this way he is treated and honoured as a thinking, rational being – as the one who is known for what he has done".[34]

What do all these speculative propositions imply? From the philosopher's standpoint, they imply that Hegel and Ehrström place, objectively or in principle or in itself,[35] a person – be he subjectively or actually or for itself[36] in his intentions a Kantian moral angel with good will as his only motive or the most wretched fellow with brutish utilitarian motives or anybody else – in the same position when the question is of the abstract justification of punishment. The very thin grounds of the preconditions of this justification are expressed in the part "Abstract Right" in *PR*, especially in paragraphs 36, 38 and 45-49.

In § 36 Hegel first says that the abstract personality of every human being as a person contains in itself the capacity for right and therefore posits the basic commandment of abstract or natural law: be a person and respect others as persons. From the point of view of legal punishment, this means penal capacity as the precondition of criminal liability.[37]

In § 38 Hegel says that precisely because of the abstractness or the abstract universality of natural law, the abstract rights of a person are limited to the negative: not to violate an individual's personality and what ensues from the individual's personality. To put it very simply, this means that the only goods (*Rechtsgüter*) natural law is expected to protect are life, physical inviolability, external freedom and, in a very unspecified way, the private or personal property of a person.[38]

Now we may understand what Ehrström means when he writes: "[i]n this way the right, which is the basic concept of all [personal] rights, differentiates itself into qualitive and quantitative determinations. In the same way, the coercion which a crime contains can be and as a matter of fact is differentiated into qualitative and quantitative determinations".

On this abstract and phenomenal level, the question is whether there can be any thing – be it a crime or anything else – which could be present without some quality and quantity. A crime without any qualitative and quantitative aspects would be a non-crime or nothing, just as, for example, a piece of private or personal property without at least one qualitative and quantitative property would not be property at all.[39]

Concerning the objective side of crime and punishment, Ehrström continues: "If we now take crime as an instance of coercion which is directed against those outwardly existing rights or against the right as existent, then it causes damage which will be cancelled through civil satisfaction in the form of compensation".[40] However, then comes another crucial point: "But as a matter of fact, crime is not only an attack against these rights... but also an attack against the right implicit in the offender himself or against the general rational will; its own positive existence crime has namely only in the arbitrary will of the offender himself".

And then, following in Hegel's footsteps, Ehrström takes again the philosopher's standpoint together with that of the legislator and the judge and imputes to the offender his infringement, which in principle or in itself is of course on this general level abstracted from and only implicitely connected to all other rights valid in other conceptual formations in *PR*:

"The coercion which the punishment contains must thus be directed against the will of the offender. It cannot, however, be reached within him but only in those rights in which his will is outwardly existent. Likewise, these rights may differentiate themselves into qualitative and quantitative determinations. Therefore the coercion which the punishment contains is also directed against one of these rights. And because the punishment or cancellation or negation of the crime is coercion against coercion, this cancellation becomes retribution: equal for equal. But this retribution is not the specific equality of the two kinds of coercion, of crime and punishment. It is equality in their value so that each crime has a punishment equal in terms of its value."[41]

One can say that Ehrström's description of Hegel's theory of punishment in the context of Abstract Right is quite accurate. But before we go on to analyse it in the somewhat larger context of *PR*, let us recapitulate Ehrström's critique of Hegel's theory.

15

Ehrström's Criticism of Hegel's Theory and Hegel's Answer

Ehrström notes accurately that for Hegel only the objective side of crime as an infringement of rights is significant, and that he disregards its subjective side, i.e. the subject's guilt. And for that reason Hegel does not extend the punishment to apply also to the cancellation of subjective wrongfulness in the offender's will for himself. Therefore one should punish, for example, crimes of negligence in the same measure as intentional crimes and unpremeditated crimes in the same measure as premeditated crimes. Ehrström acknowledges that in *PR*'s part "Morality" Hegel obviously supports the view that no one should be punished for an unintentional act; and thus it follows that Hegel recognizes that crimes of negligence should be punished more leniently than intentionally committed crimes.[42] However, according to Ehrström, Hegel forgets to apply this principle to his theory of punishment, which "leads to injustice and harshness and is actually useless in practice".

Moreover, in Ehrström's opinion Hegel's theory can be criticized by arguing that it allows deterrence, reform, the security of the state and other relative purposes to influence the execution of the sentence. But on the other hand Hegel denies that these purposes are essential elements of punishment: "[i]f namely one allows these outer purposes of punishment to have a concrete effect on the determination and execution of the punishment, one can never be sure that a punishment will be preserved as a punishment and will not be transformed into something else and thus become unjust". On these grounds Ehrström concludes: "Hegel could not prove them to be essential elements. Therefore he should not have given them significance in the execution of a punishment either."[43]

Since this appears to be a harsh critique, let us at this point see whether it is justified or not.

What is the real reason behind this negative critique? Putting aside all kinds of systematical and scholarly disputes,[44] it is in my opinion the fact that Ehrström was also a practitioner.

One must surely admire Hegel's social realism and prophetic insights into the future development of emerging nineteenth-century industrialized societies.[45] But – and that is for all practical purposes the decisive point – he could not give an ethically satisfactory or justified answer to, as he puts it, "the important question of how poverty can be remedied", poverty which according to him threatened to torment especially modern societies.

Concerning the causes of criminality Hegel writes: "Poverty in itself does not reduce people to a rabble; a rabble is created only by the disposition associated with poverty, by inward rebellion against the rich, against society, the government, etc. It follows that those who are dependent on contingency become frivolous and lazy like the Lazzaroni of Naples. This in turn gives rise to the evil that the rabble do not have sufficient honour to gain their livelihood through their work. No one can assert a right against nature, but within the conditions of society hardship at once assumes the form of wrong inflicted on this or that class."[46]

As we can see, Hegel was deeply aware of the main cause of traditional criminality as he knew it. But as a remedy against it and all kinds of other anomalies, he was basically able to suggest only the general social policy of the relatively narrow section on the Police in *PR* as well as colonization. Otherwise, one could say that *PR* is written in a very Aristotelian manner for an already educated and fairly virtuous citizen in order to elevate or even sublimate his ethical consciousness on the speculative level – in the last instance in and through the Absolute Idea as an absolute spirit[47]: "[t]o consider something rationally means not to bring reason on the object from outside in order to work upon it, for the object is itself rational for itself; it is the spirit in its freedom, the highest apex of self-conscious reason, which gives itself actuality and engenders itself as an existing world; and the sole business of science is to make conscious this work which is accomplished by the reason of the thing or matter itself."[48]

Contrary to Hegel, Ehrström very deeply understands that the formal retributive justice of the classical rule of law state and the utilitarian and integrative general prevention directed against and for the benefit of the fairly virtuous citizens as potential criminals, on the one hand, and especially the utilitarian general, special and individual prevention directed against wretched fellows as more approximately actual criminals, on the other hand, are only the formal and empirical core of rational criminal policy. And that is why he requires that the control of criminality by the empirical state needs something more for its justification than the mere speculative explication of "the voice of reason of the thing itself". In other words, he realizes and recognizes that for the vast majority of traditional criminals of bourgeois civil society "the coercion of reason" and utilitarian deterrence and treatment are not strong enough motives to prevent them from committing crimes.

Ehrström indeed acknowledges that Hegel also had something to say about the significance of the various relative or utilitarian purposes of punishment which he subsumed and treated under the term "danger to public security".[49] He even openly paraphrases Hegel's concession to limited decisionism in meting out sentences, which is expressed in *PR* in the following way: "[I]t is reason itself that recognizes that contingency, contradiction, and semblance have their (albeit limited) sphere and right, and it does not attempt to reduce such contradictions to a just equivalence; here, the only interest present is that of actualization, the interest that some kind of determination and decision should be reached, no matter how this is done (within given limits)."

The foregoing exemplifies the practical limitation of the "speculative concept" on the level of adjudication from the judge's standpoint.

Similarly, Ehrström recognizes that Hegel sets scales of penalties on the legislative level to depend on "the legislator's degree of cultivation or education" which, of course, is always relative.[50] With pleasure he finally writes the following:

"Such is Hegel's theory of punishment in broad outline. When he then applies it to society's criminal laws he observes that every crime is more or less dangerous to society. For a crime is not only an attack against the right in itself and against an individual's rights, but also an attack against the societal validity of right. In Hegel's opinion crime therefore on the one hand appears as more aggravating but on the other hand its weight diminishes in proportion to the strength of societal bonds. Therefore the higher the cultural development is, the more lenient are the criminal laws."[51]

This is Hegel's conviction and all the marketing society's utilitarian calculators of crime and punishment could learn a lot from it. But there remains the above-mentioned problem of developing a really effective means of preventing crimes, especially when one takes into account the huge recidivism rates amongst the rabble. And it is just this question Ehrström concentrates on when he criticizes Hegel for forgetting the subjective side of crime and punishment.[52]

Hegel indeed allowed punishment to have also deterrent effects on the level of legislation and adjudication and reformatory effects, particularly at the level of its execution. But as an ethical theorist he was of the opinion that it was not a matter of 'the speculative concept of punishment' to clarify and justify these in detail: "The various considerations which are relevant to punishment as phenomenon and to its relation to the particular consciousness, and which concern its effect on reprensentational thought (as deterrent, corrective or reformatory etc.), are of essential significance in their proper context, though primarily only in connection with the modality of punishment. But they take it for granted that punishment in and for itself is just."[53]

We may well ask what the word 'just' means in this context. And the answer is in itself or potentially very simple, but for itself or actually, of course, extremely complicated. In itself it means the requirement of just retribution as the deliminating factor of punishment on all levels of the practice of the criminal justice system and thus both from the legislator's and judge's as well as the executor's standpoint. In the last instance, however, it means that from the philosopher's standpoint Hegel wrote his whole book and indeed his whole encyclopaedic system to demonstrate speculatively to the phenomenological consciousness of the criminal and of all others how they must comprehend just punishment in the total context of the rationally articulated social world in *PR* in order to critically reconcile themselves with the empirical criminal justice system, too.

To describe and criticize this would of course be a task of its own. So let us finally only recapitulate the main points of Ehrström's Hegel-critique in some detail.

Ehrström criticizes Hegel for being unable to deduce the relative purposes of punishment, which are always a part of its justification, from the concept, or as Ehrström usually expresses the matter, from the essence of punishment. Deduced from this essence as a dialectic of the theories of punishment, legal punishment is demonstrated to be a means of 1) deterring the arbitrary masses from crimes, 2) of reforming the convict, and thus 3) of warranting the security of the state.

Therefore punishment also serves all the purposes for which relative or utilitarian theories have sought to justify its use.[54] But the relative theories have, of course, been unable to deduce these purposes and justification for exactly the opposite reasons from those which hold true for Hegel and the absolute theories. For the utilitarians, the state is only an institution protecting their private interests. And in the last instance, as a Hegelian absolute idealist, Ehrström sees this protective institution not to be the state proper but bourgeois civil society as a sphere of external reality and a necessity of legally mediated needs and works.[55] In this phenomenal world of the state proper, Ehrström considers it necessary from the legislator's standpoint to use deterrence or negative general prevention in order to ensure that the masses will observe law and order and from virtuous citizen's standpoint to secure the efficiency of the criminal justice system on its adjudicative level in order to justify punishment in general and in particular. However, as a Christian humanist and a dedicated practitioner, Ehrström recognizes that these do not constitute a strong and fair enough means of preventing particularly the recidivism of criminals coming from the masses or from the lower social groups. That is the reason why he speculatively deduces, or without the metaphysical spirals of Hegel-Sprache, considers it ethically more just to try to give the convict who is to be punished not only an ideal opportunity for repentance and moral regeneration but also a real chance to reform his physical and mental health, to acquire education and through the whole reformatory process change his outer conduct as well. And this, of course within the limits of just retribution, is according to him the main purpose of legal punishment as a just, efficient and human means for the criminal to live in freedom as virtuously as possible in this valley of tears.

I conclude my article with only one rebuttal from Hegel's side. In paragraph 220 of *PR* Hegel writes about the justification of punishment as practiced in civilized civil society as follows: "...and subjectively, it [the punishment] applies to the criminal in that his law, which is known by him and is valid for him and for his protection, is enforced upon him in such a way that he himself finds in it the satisfaction of justice and merely the enactment of what is proper to him".

Now, as Ted Honderich has noted, J.M.E. McTaggart for example has interpreted this passage to mean that a convict may in general be reformed by the punishment and that he claims this reformation as his right. It is not that punishment, particularly imprisonment, that provides the authorities with an opportunity to reform an offender by one means or another. It is that punishment itself, the experience of suffering or deprivation, that has a reforming effect.[56] This is an implausible interpretation, because Hegel was clearly aware that the prisons in his time were places in which the prisoners experienced endless suffering without repentance or reform.[57] But Hegel could not accept naked utilitarian reformatory treatment of the convicts either. In many passages he again and again emphasizes this point: "[Modern] human beings expect to be judged in accordance with their self-determination, and are in this respect free, whatever external determinations may be at work. It is impossible to break into this inner conviction of human beings; it is inviolable, and the moral will is therefore inaccessible."[58] And as we have already seen, he very realistically comprehended a rabble-recidivist's minimal possibilities for moral regeneration and its fulfillment in rehabilitated conduct in the practices of bourgeois civil society.

Did Hegel then have something to offer instead? Not much for the immediate empirical consciousness of the legislator, judge, executioner, convict and citizen, but a great deal for the mediating theoretical self-consciousness of his already in some measure philosophically educated reader, I would say. For the former, he can only assure with Pascal that they "will all be damned, these half-sinners who retain some love of virtue. But as for those open sinners, hardened sinners, undiluted, complete, and consummate sinners, hell cannot hold them: they have deceived the devil by their complete surrender."[59]

Therefore, say, besides honouring criminals as infinitely valuable individual persons[60] in the retributive aspect of their punishment, the commandment of right is to protect them as subjectsagainst the resentments and vindictiveness of other citizens[61] so that they can at least in principle morally regenerate themselves and show that they are reformed also in their outer conduct. Moreover, there is good reason to encourage or strengthen this regeneration process because inner conviction is a stronger motive to abide by the law and thus prevent crimes than the calculation of naked utilitarian benefit or harm. But reforming an individual convict is, according to Hegel, always a more or less contingent fact. And as we have seen, it is absolutely prohibited to use any manipulation in the reforming process.

At the theoretical level Hegel again has to offer his whole encyclopaedic system and especially *PR* as a solid outline of a person's intrinsically speculative ethical spirit which he can without any coercion comprehend for itself and then ideally or absolutely freely reconcile with himself, with other people and in the last instance with the absolute: "[t]o recognize reason as the rose in the cross of the present – this rational insight is the reconciliation with actuality which philosophy grants to those who have received the inner call to comprehend and to preserve their subjective freedom in the realm of the substantial, and at the same time to stand with their freedom not in a particular and contingent situation, but in what has being in and for itself".[62]

Ehrström, a practitioner and a Christian humanist, tries to offer to the legislator, judge and executioner more empirically determined measurement criteria concerning the objective and subjective side of crime and punishment. And in this, and only this, way he sees concrete punishment as justifiable in empirical reality as well. And because punishments should be meted out within the limits of just retribution, he believes that he has in principle excluded the risk of arbitrariness which is always connected with deterrent and especially with naked reformatory intentions. If, again, Hegel could have had the opportunity to take notice of Ehrström's in themselves very logically developed measurement criteria, he, I presume, would very likely have retained his ideal reconciliation doctrine. To put it very simply: in the transformation of the formal possibility of moral regeneration and 'therapeutic treatment' into reality, there is always a great risk of hypocrisy, of indoctrination, of the rhetoric of good intentions, of emotional hypersubjectivism, of irony and of all other kinds of human vices which Hegel criticizes with brilliant speculative rhetoric in the extensive Remarks of paragraph 140 in *PR*. These again have their ground in the fact that the subjectivity of moral actors in bourgeois civil society and empirical state – be it the subjectivity of the punishers or of the punished – "as abstract self-determination and pure certainty of itself alone, evaporates into itself all determinate aspects of right, duty and determinate being, inasmuch as its is the power of judgement which determines solely from within itself what is good in relation to the given content".[63]

To conclude: it is in principle this purely Kantian moral subject as a member of the kingdom of the ends to whom Hegel will show the way of reconciliation through various subject/object mediations in the conceptual formations of *PR*. For rabble-recidivists, this is something quite difficult to comprehend in the penal institutions of the day.

Notes

[1] I am grateful to Associate Professor Henry Fullenwider and Associate Professor Kimmo Nuotio for corrections and many valuable suggestions concerning the language of my article.

[2] H.-G. Gadamer (1976), p. 49.

[3] Hohmann (1993), Klesczewski (1990), Primoratz (1986), Tunick (1992).

[4] Ehrström is here directly dependent on Hegel. Cf. *PR* § 31 R, p. 60.

[5] Critically accepting and developing especially views of two Hegelian theorists of criminal law, Christian Reinhold Köstlin and Adolf Friedrich Berner.

[6] *Lectures*, pp. 27-28.

[7] On the main arguments of modern utilitarian deterrence and reformative theories, see T. Honderich (1989), pp. 51-87 (deterrence) and pp. 88–104 (reform); C.L. Ten (1987), pp. 7-37; N. Lacey (1988), pp. 27-46.

[8] See *Lectures* 2, p. 63.

[9] On various retributive theories, see T. Honderich, op.cit., pp. 22-50; C.L. Ten, op.cit., pp. 38-65; N. Lacey, op.cit., pp. 16-27.

[10] *Lectures*, pp. 29-30.

[11] Cf. N. Lacey, op.cit., pp. 4-12.

[12] I shall return to this point at the end of my article.

[13] *Lectures*, p. 32.

[14] A German criminal law theorist (1769-1843).

[15] A German criminal law theorist (1783-1875).

[16] It is, of course, very odd to see Kant so straightforwardly as a social contract theorist. But that is Ehrström's Hegelian heritage, which we cannot discuss here in detail. See *PR* § 75 R, pp. 105-106 and § 258 R, pp. 276-277.

[17] Lectures, pp. 52-53. See also I. Kant, *Die Metaphysik der Sitten*, pp. 452-459, especially p. 453.

[18] *Lectures*, pp. 53-56.

[19] Cf. PR§ 4, p. 36, § 118 R, p. 146, § 132, pp. 158-161 and concerning the legal process, *PR* § 227, pp. 256-257.

[20] *Lectures*, pp. 56-60.

[21] Of course, only on one or two crucial points, and for the Ladies, too.

[22] *Lectures*, p. 63. Cf. especially *PR* § 258, p. 276: "Since the state is objective spirit, it is only through being a member of the state that the individual himself has objectivity, truth, and ethical life. Union as such is itself the true content and end, and the destiny of individuals is to lead a universal life".

[23] *PR* § 75 R, p. 105, and especially § 183, p. 221, where Hegel speaks of modern civil society as "the external state, the state of necessity and of the understanding".

[24] Concerning Hegel's position see especially his polemics against Carl Ludvig von Haller in *PR* § 219 R, p. 252, and § 258 R, 278-281.

[25] *Lectures*, p. 64. Cf. *PR* § 258 A, p. 279.

[26] See also *PR* § 128, pp. 250-251. Cf. *PR* § 187, pp. 224-226.

[27] *Lectures*, p. 64. Cf. *PR* § 343 R, pp. 372-373.

[28] *Lectures*, p. 63.

[29] In the following I call the level of those "eternal laws of reason" the "philosopher's standpoint" in relation to positive law, and the level of concrete legislation the "legislator's standpoint" in relation to positive law.

[30] *Lectures*, p. 65. The pronoun "all" can be interpreted to refer to the legislator's standpoint and the pronoun "everybody" to what I shall in the following call the "citizen's standpoint" with respect to positive law.

[31] Cf. *PR* § 91, pp. 119-120: "...the free will in and for itself cannot be coerced (5 §), except in so far as it fails to withdraw itself from the external dimension in which it is caught up, or from its idea of the latter. Only he who wills to be coerced can be coerced into anything."

[32] *Lectures*, pp. 65-66.

[33] *Lectures*, p. 66. Cf. *PR* § 95, pp. 121-122, § 97, p. 123, § 99, p. 124.

[34] *Lectures*, pp. 66-68. Cf. *PR* § 36, p. 69, § 99 R, pp. 124-125, § 100, p. 126, § 220, p. 252.

[35] In German: "an sich" or "für uns" as philosophers.

[36] In German: "für sich".

[37] See in more detail *PR* § 120, pp. 148-149 and § 132 R, pp. 158-161.

[38] See *PR* § 45-49, pp. 77-80.

[39] From the point of view of the scale of penalties this differentiated level can be called the "judge's standpoint". Hegel deals with it briefly in *PR* § 214, pp. 245-246.

[40] Cf. *PR* § 98, p. 124.

[41] *Lectures*, pp. 69-71. Cf. *PR* § 99, pp. 124-125, § 100, p. 126, and especially § 101, pp. 127-129.

[42] See *PR* § 96 R, p. 123, § 117-120, pp. 144-149, § 132, pp. 158-161.

[43] *Lectures*, pp. 73-75.

[44] In my doctoral dissertation, which will be published in 1997, I discuss the influence of the German Hegelian criminal law theorists and especially J.V. Snellman on Ehrström's development in these matters.

[45] See, for example, *PR* § 243-246, pp. 266-268. Cf. § 49, pp. 79-81, § 200, pp. 233-234.

[46] *PR* § 244 A, pp. 266-267, and from the point of view of coercion directed against the rabble, see T. Airaksinen (1988), pp. 15-22.

[47] See especially *PR* § 29-32, pp. 58-62, and, from the viewpoint of ethical and political justification, the very relevant paragraphs § 150-157, pp. 193-198, § 260-261, pp. 282-285 and § 268, pp. 288-289.

[48] *PR* § 31, p. 60.
[49] See *PR* § 96, p. 123, § 99-101, pp. 124-129, § 218, pp. 250-251.
[50] *Lectures*, pp. 71-72. Cf. *PR* § 101 R, p. 128, § 187, pp. 224-226, § 214, pp. 245-246.
[51] *Lectures*, p. 72. Cf. especially *PR* § 218 A, p. 251.
[52] This could be called the "executor's standpoint".
[53] *PR* § 99 R, p. 125.
[54] *Principle*, p. 94.
[55] *Principle*, p. 89.
[56] See T. Honderich, op.cit., p. 48.
[57] See, for example, Ilt 4, p. 580.
[58] *PR* § 106 A, 136.
[59] *PR* § 140, p. 171 and pp. 177-178.
[60] Cf. *PR* § 36, p. 60, § 209, p. 240.
[61] Cf. *PR* § 102-103, pp. 130-131 and § 221, p. 253.
[62] *PR*, Preface, p. 22. Cf. especially *PR* § 23, p. 54 and M.O. Hardimon (1994), pp. 95-119.
[63] *PR* § 138, p. 166.

References

Airaksinen,T. 1988. *Ethics of Coercion and Authority: A Philosophical Study of Social Life.*University of Pittsburgh Press.

Ehrström, K.G. 1860-1861. *Föreläsningar öfver Kriminalrättens allmänna del, Enligt Berner.* [Lectures on the General Part of Criminal Law from the Spring Semester 1860 to the Spring Semester 1861, Based on Berner]. HYK [University Library of Helsinki] Bö II 1. (Lectures)

Ehrström, K.G. 1994. *Föreläsningar över straffrättens allmänna läror.* Redigerat samt med förord, biografi, bibliografi och anmärkningar försett: Markus Wahlberg. Publikationer från institutionen för straff- och processrätt vid Helsingfors universitet A:7. Helsingfors 1994. [Lectures on General Doctrines of Criminal Law. Edited with Foreword, Biography, Bibliography and Footnotes by Markus Wahlberg. Publisher: Department of Criminal Law and Judicial Procedure at the University of Helsinki. 1994] (Lectures 2)

Ehrström, K.G. 1859. *Om principen för fängelsestraffets ordnande.* [On the Principle for Organizing Prison as Penalty]. Helsingfors. Frenckell & Son. (Principle)

Gadamer, H.-G. 1976. *Hegel's Dialectic. Five Hermeneutical Studies.* Yale University Press.

Hardimon, M.O. 1994. *Hegel's Social Philosophy. The Project of Reconciliation.* Cambridge University Press.

Hegel, G.W.F. 1991 (1820). *Elements of the Philosophy of Right.* Cambridge Texts in the History of Political Thought. Cambridge University Press. (*PR*; R=Remarks; A=Addition)

Hohmann, R. 1993. *Personalität und strafrechtliche Zurechnung.* Frankfurt am Main: Peter Lang.

Honderich, T. 1989. *Punishment. The Supposed Justifications.* Polity Press.

Ilting, K.-H. 1974. *"Hegels Philosophie des Rechts" nach der Vorlesungsnachschrift K.G. Griesheims 1824/25.* Vorlesungen über Rechtsphilosophie 1818-1831 IV. Stuttgart-Bad Canstatt: Frommann Verlag. (Ilt 4)

Kant, I. 1977. (1797/98). *Die Metaphysik der Sitten.* Werkausgabe Band VIII. Hrsg. von W. Weischedel. Suhrkamp Taschenbuch Wissenschaft 190.

Klesczewski, D. 1990. *Die Rolle der Strafe in Hegels Theorie der bürgerlichen Gesellschaft.* Berlin: Duncker & Humboldt.

Lacey, N. 1988. *State Punishment. Political Principles and Community Values.* London and New York: Routledge.

Primoratz, I. 1986. Banquos Geist. Hegels Theorie der Strafe. *Hegel-Studien Beiheft 29.* Bonn: Bouvier Verlag.

Ten, C.L. 1987. *Crime, Guilt, and Punishment.* Clarendon Press.

Tunick, M. 1992. *Hegel's Political Philosophy.* Princeton University Press.

Tuija Pulkkinen

MORALITY IN HEGEL'S PHILOSOPHY OF RIGHT

Johan Vilhelm Snellman, a political leader in Finland during the last century as well as a serious Hegel-scholar, stressed morality in his interpretation of Hegel's *Elements of the Philosophy of Right* (*PR*). The middle section "Morality" of the tripartite Hegelian *PR* was his special interest, and he emphasized the topics of this section strongly in his presentation of the third section "Sittlichkeit".[1]

Snellman's definition of the state is clearly non-institutional[2] and connected with ethics. For him "the state" refers to the totality of actions of a special kind. These actions are characterized by being based on the individual's moral judgement, or as Snellman phrases it, "taking the norm for the right from within oneself". The state as a group of actions is opposed to the totality of actions called the "Civil Society". This is action which takes the existing law and customs as the norm for right conduct. The Civil Society is law-abiding society, while the state is the process of changing the laws and customs.

Snellman's concept of the state includes the idea of a politically active intellectual who identifies with the nation conceived as gen-

eral will. The term "civil society", in turn, refers to social action
where this type of commitment is not present. The concepts of "duty"
and "conscience" also have an important function in this ethico-
political system.[3]

Has Snellman departed from Hegel in a substantial way? It is
often stated that in Hegel's text the individual moral agent vanishes
and that the theme of the section "Morality" is completely lost in the
concept of "Sittlichkeit". The accusation is that Hegel's ethics is
nothing but a reinforcement of the existing social norm structure and
that Hegel's social philosophy is actually sociology without any moral
content.[4] It has even been argued that "Hegel's view is a negation
of all ethical views. It submits the individual to the collective and
'ought' to 'is'." (Anguelov 1989, 205) On the other hand, the same
interpretation of vanising morality has been given a positive emphasis in the Marxian tradition, where it has been taken as a proof of
Hegel's submission of ethics to politics (Bloch 1951; Lukács 1948,
Marcuse 1941). Some contemporary Hegel-scholars, such as
Andreas Wildt, have remarked that historically there has never been
a great interest in questions of autonomy and morality among
Hegelians (Wildt 1982, 32).

The core of the question and the way it is usually phrased is
Hegel's relation to Kant's ethics. Does Hegel oppose the Kantian
notion of moral autonomy and if so, in what way?

I

Joachim Ritter's well-known interpretation lays emphasis on the fact
that while Kant connects morality to the individual and the inner life
(*Innerlichkeit*), Hegel with his idea of *Sittlichkeit* strives to bring
together the conflict between individual and community. Hegel's point
of reference here is the ideal of the classical polis. However, Ritter
also argues that

If Hegel's philosophy is seen as being not respectful of individuality and as adoring the state, this is based on not realizing the nature of "sublation" [Aufheben] as preserving.Hegel's reception of Kantian morality has a profound and constitutive effect for his notions of "right" and "the state. (Ritter 1975, 219)

Dieter Henrich makes a similar point:

In the background of the idealist moral philosophy there is the one and only principle: it was Kant who first shaped the thought of the autonomy of reason and Hegel was the last who's idea of "Sittlichkeit" is based on it. (Henrich 1982, 7)

What happens in the section "Morality", and how is it sublated to *Sittlichkeit*? In sublation [*Aufhebung*], as T.M Knox phrases it, "The later stages cancel the earlier ones, and yet at the same time the earlier ones are absorbed within the later as moments or elements within them"(*PR*, X). This always leaves room for interpretation, because of the two seemingly contradictory moves of canceling and preserving. The history of Hegel-reception, with its radically different interpretations of what Hegel actually meant, provides ample evidence of this.

If the question is how Hegel treats Kantian morality, one has to start from another contested area by giving meaning to the notion of Kantian morality.

I offer the following reading of Kant's moral philosophy. Kant notes that humans make special kind of judgements. These judgements are not made on the basis of one's *own interest*, but on *moral* grounds. Kant's question is: what does this special quality of "morality" consist of? When the special group of judgements called moral judgements is looked at closely, he notes, it is seen that they all are of a certain form. The form is that of the "categorical imperative": in making a judgement of this kind, the agent asks himself to act so that the maxim of this action could be a universal law.

One way of interpreting the categorical imperative is simply that moral action involves the use of intellectual capacity. Another interpretation is that Kant actually claims that a moral action is based on a rule of non-contradictoriness.

Regardless of the way the categorical imperative is interpreted (and on the basis of Kant's text it is possible to defend several readings), the main point for me is to see it as a *description* of morality. I will not consider here at all the literature which takes Kant's discussion on the categorical imperative to be prescriptive and turns the categorical imperative into a rule *for* moral conduct instead of a rule *of* moral conduct.

The essential point in Kant's moral thinking, and the one that distinguishes it from vast amount of moral theorizing, is his initial statement that humans *do make* moral judgements. This is stated as a *fact*.[5]

According to Kant, the facticity of morality as a human capacity means that humans are members in the "empire of freedom". Humans have a dual citizenship. As physical creatures they are members of the "empire of necessity", which means that their existence is describable by the laws of nature. But in addition to being physical objects, they are also creatures in the "realm of freedom", i.e. they have a capacity to judge morally.[6] The same capacity is called "autonomy". The Kantian autonomy consists of this empty capacity; it does not prescribe any specific moral content. The form of this empty capacity is that of reflection. The Protestant Kantian moral agent is a subject turned to itself in an act of self-observation and self-command.

Because it is grounded on the distinction between necessity (physicality) and freedom (moral capacity), the notion of autonomy establishes a sharp opposition between, on the one hand, human natural tendencies, inclinations and desires, and, on the other hand, morality.

The Kantian vocabulary of moral autonomy also includes the notions of abstract "duty" and "conscience". The duty is the duty to use moral capacity, and the notion of conscience names the site of moral judging.

What happens, in connection with this Kantian moral vocabulary, in the section "Morality" of Hegel's *PR*? What does Hegel propose and what does he oppose? And what happens to morality, so defined, in the section on "Sittlichkeit", especially in its third sub-section, "the State"?

Hegel presents morality as the standpoint of "will"; as a standpoint of "subjectivity;" and as a standpoint of "ought", "demand", "consciousness" and "ends" (*PR* § 105-114).

The section "Morality" is divided into three sub-sections. The first deals with *purpose* and *responsibility* (culpability), i.e. an individual's right to be considered an accountable agent of an action.

This simple beginning is very significant because it means that Hegel's starting point is, indeed, that of Kantian facticity *vis-à-vis* the moral nature of human action. The first sub-section defines human action as having the quality of morality in the Kantian sense.

As the beginning of a social theory, this is radically different from the starting point of authors from the liberal tradition, who take as their initial assumption a "state of nature" among individuals and proceed to ask, prescriptively, about the social rules which establish morality. For Hegel as for Kant, morality is always there, connected with humanness and selfhood.

The second sub-section is about *intention* and about *welfare* as an aim. By including welfare in the content of the moral deed, Hegel is arguing against Kant's sharp distinction between "natural tendencies" and morality.[7] According to Hegel, satisfying "natural" needs and enjoyment may be included in a purpose which is moral. Pursuing one's own welfare and that of others, as content, is not to be separated, *per se*, from morality as the form of action.

In the third sub-section, Hegel sets himself the task of raising the subjective purpose and aim of welfare to generality. He does this by means of the *Idea of Good* (as an actualization of best possible for all) which is connected with the subjective willing of Good comprised in the notion of *Conscience*. The Good is an Idea that combines the concept of Will and a particular will. The good is connected with the rational faculty. The moral Good is represented by an individual agent (subject), who is in possession of a thinking will, free of private interest.

The basic skeleton of the section on morality shows that Hegel defines morality in very Kantian terms. Still, a lot has been written on "Hegel's critique of Kantian morality". What does this critique consist of?

I mentioned the critique implied in the notion of welfare. More comes up in Hegel's discussion of *duty*. He takes up the notion of "duty" with explicit reference to Kant. He reminds us of the formal, abstract nature of Kant's notion of duty "as the universal abstract essentiality of the will". He notes that Kant does not talk about specific duties and warns that if this autonomy is adhered to exclusively, without making the transition to Sittlichkeit, only "empty formalism" is gained.

Can this be called Hegel's critique of Kant's moral theory? He writes: "It is the merit of Kantian philosophy and its powerful view in the sphere of the practical (philosophy) to take up the role of duty." (*PR* § 133] But Hegel is not content with Kant's abstract notion of duty. He looks for a doctrine of duty which defines duty as specific, as an effect of the structure of the community and the individual's position in this community. This view, inspired by Aristotle, is the point of comparison in his criticism.

What is important to note here is that Hegel does not argue against Kant's idea of the facticity of moral autonomy and its formal analysis into the categorical imperative and the notion of duty. What he argues against is an attempt to make this description function as the sole basis of prescription. Hegel simply says that even if we know the inner structure of moral action and respect individual moral judgement, this does not enable us to know what is right and wrong or good and bad behaviour in particular instances. For that we also need to pay attention to the current social norm structure.

Another instance of Hegel's critical voice in the section "Morality" concerns the notion of *conscience*. According to Hegel, it is conscience which determines and makes the decision about right and good. Conscience is the deep feeling of being convinced of what is good and what is one's duty. For Hegel, conscience is apparently a meaningful concept, and he includes it in his system. Again, Hegel starts from the Kantian notion, gives it a central position, and by doing this, accepts the idea of morality as essentially inner. At the same time he nevertheless presents a lengthy and meticulous critique of accepting private conviction as the sole criterion when judging what is right and wrong. His critique of the "In my heart I know this is right/wrong" type of moral argumentation goes on for several pages and involves such notions as "Hypocrisy" and "Ironic consciousness". (*PR* § 138 ff.)

Once again, I would say that Hegel's critique is directed against the attempt to change the Kantian description into a prescription. Instead of saying that humans *make* moral judgements on the basis of their conscience, the advocats of inner morality say that people *should* make moral judgements on the basis of their inner conviction. For Hegel, the inner conviction is a necessary but not a suffient condition of a moral act. For the thinkers he is arguing against, it is a suffient condition.

Hegel refers here to the state of mind which emphasizes the good intention while being aware of the fact that an act might be against existing social norms and laws or causing evil. Hegel describes different forms of this type of thought as either mere hypocrisy with regard to a particular deed, or as setting oneself up as good, conscientious, and pious in the eyes of others, or as a conviction that good will is enough to make an action good. He mentions a theft "in order to do good to the poor", and a murder "out of hate or revenge" or "in order to uproot the evil". (*PR* § 140 d) The ultimate form of this sentiment is what he calls "irony", where the individual subject consciously thinks of himself as being above or beyond the existing law and order which is only for others.

Hegel's animated tone in this discussion suggests that the adversaries are contemporary and the issues are political. Indeed, this is probably the case. What Hegel is dealing here with is the social thought and practice inspired by the German Romantics. More specifically, much of this criticism seems to be targeted at romantic justifications of something which we might today call terrorism. Hegel mentions Schiller's "Bandits" where heroes would murder and steal in order to redistribute wealth and uproot the causes of evil.[8]

For Hegel, the solution to the problem of bad action based on inner conviction and crimes committed in the name of moral reasoning raised above the conventional is the move toward societal structures of morality. Subjectivity cannot be conceived as the final court of appeal. For Hegel, the structure of internal moral judgment needs to be complemented by an analysis of social institutions in order to have a complete picture of issues involved in moral judging.

If the social order and existing norms and laws have to be respected in properly moral behaviour, do we then fall back on the view that Hegel has been accused of? Is this a doctrine for preserving the existing social order? Is Hegel in favor of "is" against "ought"?

The relationship between "is" and "ought" in Hegel is not a simple one and is connected to his philosophical system in its entirety. Yet, it would be very wrong to say that he reduces"ought" to "is" – rather the opposite could be claimed: all "is" becomes "ought". Odo Marquard, for example, has noted that "ought" and "is" cannot be separated in Hegel's system. Hegel's great idea was, according to Marquard, that all philosophy is practical philosophy. At the end of *The Science of Logic*, in the passage on will and knowledge, Hegel notes that spirit (the human sphere) cannot be approached as nature because, since spirit is spirit observing itself, which makes it unavoidable that in this observation "ought" is always present. Here we encounter again the profoundly Kantian nature of Hegelian reasoning. Because humanness is always connected with morality and morality is the standpoint of "ought," the "ought" is connected with the "is" of the human sphere. The being of spirit is saturated with "ought", which is not in Hegel a result of the internal teleology of things as it would be in the Aristotelian model, but a result of human autonomy. The capacity for morality follows humans and is woven unavoidably into human existence. As Marquard says: Hegel's philosophy is practical through and through. In other words, Hegel does not in his presentation differentiate between description and prescription. His writing is descriptive-prescriptive; descriptive and prescriptive simultaneously.

On the basis of the discussion this far, we may already conclude that it is clearly wrong to present Hegel as mainly a critic of Kantian ethics, or devoid of morality in the Kantian sense. On the contrary, Hegel clearly starts from the assumption of human autonomy in the Kantian sense and bases his social thought on this foundation. Furthermore, I would argue that the Kantian idea of subjectivity as morally self-reflective is a necessary means for understanding Hegel's doctrine of the state.

II

The next question is: what is the function of morality in the later stages of description-prescription in Hegel's *PR*? The discussion of the section on morality leaves us with several ideas: that of a moral agent as a will in control of itself, of duty as a detailed duty, of good as everybody's well-being and of conscience as a feeling of being internally convinced.

Skipping over the first two sections of "Sittlichkeit" (The Abstract Right and The Civil Society), I proceed to see how morality, in these terms, is caught up in the section on state. As a prescription-description, The State simultaneously describes existing states and a state as it ought to be, not universally, but at the time and place of Hegel's writing. The State that Hegel presents is built on its members' trust that their own and other's well-being is taken care of by it. In the state, individuals have specific duties, which come with their specific position in the society. By living their specific lives dutifully, they take part in creating everybody's well-being. The agent (subject) which wills the common good is the state.

The State is a will. Hegel gives Rousseau credit for realising that will is a principle of the state. The state is the general will, an agent which legislates for itself, i.e. sets its own norms, consciously and rationally. The general will is separate from the will of all and it is separate from the will of the individual(s) in power. As such it is an abstraction.[12]

In the first paragraph of the section on the State, Hegel writes: [The State]... is ethical mind qua the substantial will manifest and revealed to itself, knowing and thinking itself, accomplishing what it knows ..." (*PR* § 257). The state is a willing mind.

I would pay attention to the fact that the idea of moral agency (moral subjectivity) is transferred from the section "Morality" into the section "Sittlichkeit" in the form of *the general will*. The form of the state as a general will is that of a Kantian self-legislating, self-reflexive, moral self. The state is here conceived as a form of a consciousness, a subject comparable in structure to human consciousness with faculties of knowing and willing.

Self-reflexivity is the essential quality of the nation-state conceived as a subject. It is a subject in command of itself. The state is supposed to legislate in a self-reflexive mode, according to morality which is already present in the nation.

There are also other ideas that are transferred. The abstract good as the aim of the will re-emerges as the aim/goal of the state subject; and this goal is the well-being of all. The conviction (being convinced) of the conscience comes up in the section on The State as the conviction of the citizens of the goodness of the state (trust).

Hegel's modern state is a prescription-description of a constitutional state (which most German states of his time were not); it guarantees the representations of separate interest groups, the freedom of opinion formation and the freedom to express opinions. The division of positions in society among individuals has to be based on individuals' free choice of their places. These are requirements of specifically *modern* subjectivity that according to Hegel is not present in the ancient polis or in Plato's ideal state. Hegel writes:

> The principle of the modern state has this incredible strength and depth: it lets the principle of subjectivity be fullfilled up to the independent extreme of its personal specificity and simultaneously it brings it back to the substantial unity and in this way makes it stay with itself. (*PR* § 260)

In this view, an individual should feel that her personal goals concerning values and well-being are cared for in the state. Hegel goes on:

> It has often been stated that the goal of the state is the happiness of its citizens; this is certainly true; if the citizens are not happy, if their personal goals do not get fullfilled or if they do not

38

feel state to be a mediator in this fullfillment, then the state is in no good condition. (*PR* § 265)

The themes of "*Subjektivität*", selfhood, and agency recur in *PR*. Subjectivity – a consciousness which is a will, reflexive and legislating for itself – is, according to Hegel, the product of Christianity and the principle which separates modernity from the ancient world. The Kantian morally autonomous subject is at the heart of Hegel's concept of modernity. This is why morality occupies such a central place in Hegel's *Sittlichkeit*.

III

Returning to Snellman, we may note his differences from Hegel. Both make the issues of the section "Morality" to re-emerge in the section on the state, but in a different way. Snellman is interested in developing a doctrine of duty *in abstracto*. For him, the duty of an individual is to act morally. The state is the sphere where the individual, listening to his conscience, identifies himself with the general will and judges as the general will (the nation) would judge. Hegel, in his turn, does not present the moral action of an individual as immeadiately approximating or identifying with the state's will. For him the state (as an abstract subjecthood) remains in a position of a mediator for private morality. The organisation of the state serves as the individual's means of fulfilling his duties and rights. As a moral agent, he is supposed to do this with conscience and aiming at everyone's well-being.

The themes of Kantian morality (will, subjectivity, duty, conscience and internal conviction) are also present in Hegel, re-emerging in an individual's relationship to the state and in the presentation of the state itself. The domain of "Sittlichkeit", in its entirety, is a conglomeration of moral decisions, which are constantly being reinforced by moral conviction and trust. This means that the idea of moral autonomy grounds the entire sphere of Sittlichkeit. Hegel is critical about interpreting the categorical imperative or the abstract notion of duty prescriptively. However, the idea of moral autonomy, the idea of human subjectivity as a rational agent with a will, is deeply embedded in Hegel's philosophy. Just as T.M. Knox, his English translator, has remarked: "Hegel is in his ethics a Kantian in some fundamental way."

Notes

[1] The difficulties in translating various Hegelian notions, among them "Sittlichkeit", are notorious. The problem with the standard English translation, "Ethical Life" (Knox), is that it loses the social flavor of "Sitten" (mores, habits, manners, or existing social norm structures), which is so central to "Sittlichkeit". Steven Smith, in *Hegel's Critique of Liberalism*, uses "the institutions of ethical life," which is more accurate but, of course, too clumsy to be a standard translation.

Snellman (1806-1881), who wrote in Swedish, used the term "sedlighet", which is derived from "sed", an almost exact counterpart to the German "Sitte". An anthropologist might, for example, talk about "sitten" or "seder" of a distant tribe when observing their way of living. In Finnish, the equivalent word would be "tapa" (s) or "tavat" (pl)" (mores, habits, manners); but unfortunately the noun derived from it, "tavallisuus", already has another, established meaning. It means ordinariness or usualness, so that a person who is "tavallinen" is not "one who follows social norms" but "somebody who is not interesting". When Snellman's texts were translated into Finnish in 1929-1933, the term used for "Sittlichkeit" was "siveellisyys", which in contemporary language means something like "prudishness" and has caused some unfortunate confusions.

Hegel, of course, uses "Sittlichkeit" in distinction to "Moralität", which in the postkantian German philosophy has no connection to the social life but instead to "Innerlichkeit", the inner life of an individual. Hegel's aim to bring together the individual and the community, morality and legality has usually been recognized by commentators, and the connection that this enterprise has with his interest in the classics, especially Aristotle, has often been noted.

[2] The non-institutional definition of the state matches the historical conditions of its emergence. At the time Snellman was writing, the "Fin-

nish State" was mentioned frequently even if, strictly speaking, nothing of the kind existed. As an autonomous Grand Duchy, Finland was part of the Russian Empire, and did not gain the status of an independent state until 1917.

[3] In 1839 Snellman published a book for students on the Hegelian philosophy of right, entitled *Elementarkurs i rättslära*. He followed Hegel in structure and style but altered the presentation on points of philosophical disagreement. In 1844 he published another, much longer presentation on the same subject, this time in the hope of getting a larger audience. However, *Läran om Staten* never became a bestseller. It was, as everything Snellman wrote, a systematic presentation in the heavy Hegelian mode. After ten years of political engagement, Snellman returned to the academy in 1856 and lectured on philosophy until 1863. His manuscripts of these lectures, about 5 000 pages, have been stored in the Helsinki University Library and are currently in the process of being published with commentaries in the new 12-volume *Samlade arbeten* (Collected works).

[4] This line of criticism is very clearly stated, for example, in Walsh (1969).

[5] My emphasis here differs slightly from that of Allen Wood, who says of Hegel's ethics that "Like Kantian ethics, it is based on the value of freedom and rational selfhood". I would say "on the facticity of freedom and rational selfhood".

[6] At the very beginning of the Preface for *Grundlegung der Metaphysik der Sitten*, Kant presents Ethics as a science which explores the "laws of freedom" just as physics explores the "laws of nature". This states very clearly the facticity and descriptive nature of his enterprise.

[7] Especially in paragraph 124: "... like the view that, in willing, objective and subjective ends are mutually exclusive, is an empty dogmatism of the abstract Understanding."

[8] The problem is the same that Fedor Dostoyevski takes up in *Crime and Punisment*: should not the good and conscientious student, Roskolnikov, who has a future, be entitled to murder a rich old landlady, who is the cause of a lot of evil for those around her. He would uproot the evil and help himself, who is undeservingly poor. Or the same that Jean-Francois Lyotard, who also reflects on the Kantian moral theory, confronts in *Just Gaming* by judging contemporary terrorist acts which are made in the name of social justice. For Lyotard, terrorists are the Red Brigades murdering corporate magnates, for Hegel they are bandits who murder aristocrats.

Hegel and Lyotard converge in critically considering not only justification for terrorism but also for terror. For Hegel this is the terror of the Jacobins of the French Revolution; for Lyotard the terror of the Nazis, Stalin or Pol Pot. Both Hegel and Lyotard have a serious relationship to the revolutionary and romantic tradition.

[9] Quentin Skinner calls this a "double abstraction" view of the state.

References

Anguelov, Stephane (1983) Sur les conceptions éthiques de Hegel. *Annalen der internationalen Gesellschaft für dialektische Philosophie. Societas Hegeliana Jahrbuch 193*. Pahl-Rugenstein. Köln.

Avineri, Shlomo (1976) *Hegel's Theory of the Modern State*. Cambridge University Press, Cambridge.

Bloch, Ernst (1962) *Subjekt-Objekt. Erläuterungen zu Hegel*. Suhrkamp, Frankfurt/M.

Hegel, G.W.F (1969) Hegel's Science of Logic. Translated by A.V. Miller. Muirhead Library of Philosophy. Georg Allen & Unwin ltd. &Humanities Press. London-New York.

Hegel's Philosophy of Right (1969). Translated with notes by T.M. Knox. Oxford University press, London, Oxford & New York.

Henrich, Dieter (1982) *Selbstverhältnisse. Gedanken auf Auslegungen zu der Grundlagen der klassischen deutschen Philosophie*. Reclam, Stuttgart.

Ilting, Karl-Heinz (1984) The Structure of Hegel's Philosophy of Right. In Pelczynski (ed) *Hegel's* ....

Knox, T.M. (1957/58) Hegel's Attitude to Kant's Ethics. *Kant-Studien*. Band 49, Heft 1, 70-81. Köln.

Lùkacs, Georg (1973) *Der junge Hegel*. Band I. Suhrkamp, Ulm.

Lyotard, Jean-Francois & Thébaud Jean-Loup (1979) *Au juste*. Christian Bourgois, Paris.

Marcuse, Herbert (1969) *Reason and Revolution. Hegel and the Rise of Social Theory*. Beacon Press, Boston.

Marquard, Odo (1982) *Hegel und Sollen. Schwierigkeiten mit der Geschichtsphilosophie*. Suhrkamp, Frankfurt am Main.

Materialen zu Hegel's Rechtsphilosophie. Band 2. Hrg von Manfred Riedel. Suhrkamp, Frankfurt am Main 1975.

Pelczynski Z.A. (ed) (1984). *The State and Civil Society. Studies in Hegel's Political Philosophy*. Cambridge University Press, Cambridge.

Peperzaak, Adrian (1982) Hegel's Pflichten- und Tugendlehre. *Hegel-Studien*. Band 17.

Pulkkinen, Tuija (1989) *Valtio ja vapaus*. Tutkijaliitto, Helsinki.

Smith, Steven B. (1989) *Hegel's Critique of Liberalism. Rights in Context*. The University of Chicago Press, Chicago & London.

Rameil, Udo (1981) Sittlicher Sein und Subjectivität. Zur Genesis des Begriffs der Sittlichkeit in Hegels Rechtsphilosophie. *Hegel-Studien*. Band 16.

Riedel, Manfred (1969) *Studien zu Hegel's Rechtsphilosophie*. Suhrkamp, Frankfurt am Main.

Ritter, Joachim (1975) Moralität und Sittlichkeit. Zu Hegel's Auseinendersetzung mit der kantischen Ethik. *Materialen zu...* 217-243.

Siep, Ludvig (1982) Was heisst "Aufhebung der Moralität in Sittlichkeit" in Hegel's Rechtsphilosophie? *Hegel-Studien*. Band 17.

Snellman, J.V. (1992) Philosophisk elementar-curs. Tredje häftet. Rättslara. *Samlade arbeten II*, pp. 92-151. Edita, Helsinki.

Snellman, J.V. (1996-7) Manuscripts for lectures in Sedelära 1856-1863. Forthcoming in *Samlade arbeten VII, VIII and IX*.

Taylor, Charles (1979) *Hegel and Modern Society*. Cambridge University Press, Cambridge.

Walsh, W.H. (1969) *Hegelian Ethics*. Macmillan, London.

Wildt, Andreas (1982) Autonomie und Anerkennung. Hegel's Moralitätskritik im Lichte seiner Fichte-Rezeption. *Deutschen Idealismus*, Bd. 7. Klett-Cotta, Stuttgart.

Wolff, R-P. (1973) *The Autonomy of Reason. A Commentary of the Metaphysics of Morals*. Harper & Row, New York.

Wood, Allen W. (1990) *Hegel's Ethical Thought*. Cambridge University Press, Cambridge.

Michael Quante

PERSONAL AUTONOMY AND THE STRUCTURE OF THE WILL

A quarter of a century ago the concepts of personal autonomy and the will became a main theme in analytical philosophy with the publication of the now famous papers *Acting freely* by Gerald Dworkin and *Freedom of the Will and the Concept of a Person* by Harry G. Frankfurt.[1] Both developed independently similar theories analyzing the autonomy of persons in – as Marina A.L. Oshana has characterized it – a naturalistic mode ([12]). The core idea of Dworkin, Frankfurt and their followers is that free agency, autonomy of persons or freedom of the will has to be analyzed in terms of a hierarchical structure of desires or volitions, or, as it has been labeled later, in terms of the "Split-Level-Self". These new and powerful proposals have called forth a broad and fruitful discussion: the new accounts were confronted – as is usual in analytical philosophy – with "puzzle cases" which enabled the participants to make their concepts and definitions more precise. In this context some contributors like Susan Wolf ([26]) or Thomas E. Hill ([10]) introduced models of autonomy which include a revival of some

Kantian themes and theses. This is not surprising, as Kant is one of the great champions of autonomy and such a resort to Kant is not unusual in analytical philosophy. It is equally unsurprising, that there is little or no resort to the philosophy of Hegel in this discussion. This, too, I would suggest, accords with usual practice in analytical philosophy.

One and a half centuries before Dworkin and Frankfurt developed their accounts Hegel published his *Elements of the Philosophy of Right,* which included his theory of free agency and autonomy. Through his particular philosophical method and his in some parts very special terminology Hegel unfolds a theory of the will which encompasses many elements of our contemporary accounts and which answers some of the problems Split-Level-Self theories and Neo-Kantian theories are confronted with.

In Hegel's philosophy each part of the system is connected to every other part and all is governed by his special "spekulative Methode" which is developed and justified in his *Science of Logic.* As Hegel everywhere in his system says the final foundation of his method and his philosophical theses can be found there. A "top-down" approach to the study of Hegel would give a reconstruction of his *Science of Logic* and its claim to having discovered an *absolute* foundation (*Letztbegründung*).[2] Such a direct approach to Hegel's philosophy is extremely difficult and attempting it here would, I confess, be asking too much. In what follows I will try to illustrate a more indirect way of understanding Hegel's theory of the will which will also function as a *partial* defence of it.[3] In my view this "bottom-up" approach to Hegel's philosophy is justified because in that way the viability of his philosophical method can be demonstrated by showing how it works in dealing with special philosophical problems. If it can be shown that Hegel's method is able to give a plausible account of some important philosophical topic we can then show that his "spekulative Methode" has to be taken seriously and should be studied more carefully. And even if a redemption of *all* of Hegel's claims in his philosophical system can't be an option we may, nevertheless, still gain a lot through this "bottom-up" approach. That is, an interpretation of Hegel's arguments about a special philosophical problem will help us to understand two things better – Hegel's way of thinking on the one hand and the nature of the philosophical problem at issue on the other.

For our purposes I will try to understand Hegel's analysis of the will, as it is given in his *Elements of the Philosophy of Right*, as an answer to those problems which are discussed in contemporary debates about the nature of personal autonomy and its connection to the freedom of actions and the will.

In the first part I will make a brief sketch of the contemporary debates (I). In the second part I will outline Hegel's theory of personal autonomy and the structure of the will (II). I will try to show, how his theory deals with problems which crop up in the modern approaches. My main interest here is to show that Hegel has dealt with problems which still concern us; my main thesis being, that he has given some answers which remain today very much worth discussing in the context of our contempory debates on freedom and autonomy. In the final third part some specific problems of Hegel's account are discussed briefly (III).

I

In her paper *Autonomy Naturalized* Marina A.L. Oshana discusses three modern conceptions of personal autonomy which – according to her – offer "thoughtful conceptions of personal autonomy" ([12], 77) and "rid it of the metaphysical baggage that attaches to more traditional, Kantian-like conceptions" (ibid.) by naturalizing the concept of autonomy. *Naturalization*, of course, is everywhere these days – and naturalizing something is synonymous with showing that it is vivid, useful and substantial. But unfortunately, the label "naturalizing" has many different meanings and can be part of very different philosophical strategies. For our purposes Oshana's "local" concept of naturalization will suffice. She formulates two necessary conditions "a naturalized conception of autonomy must satisfy" (ibid.) which, taken together, are sufficient for naturalization:

(N1) The properties which constitute autonomy must be natural properties, knowable through the senses or by introspection (or must supervene on natural properties).

(N2) The properties that constitute autonomy must not be restricted to phenomena "internal" to the agent. In addition, certain objective, "external" properties are required.

According to Oshana the contemporary accounts of personal autonomy are naturalistic in so far as they satisfy condition (N1), but unfortunately most of them fail to satisfy condition (N 2), because they only analyze personal autonomy in purely internal terms.

Everyone who has studied Hegel's *Elements of the Philosophy of Right* and everyone who knows only a little about Hegel's criticism of Kant's moral philosophy can see that the second condition will be met by *his* theory of autonomy. In regard to the first condition a lot depends on the concept of "natural property" and on the particular analysis of "introspection". As we will see Hegel meets in some sense the first condition, too. But Hegel wouldn't accept this as naturalization if that were to imply an opposition to metaphysics. And surely Hegel also wouldn't accept an analysis of "introspection" in terms of knowledge by the senses only. But before I come to discuss these more Hegelian matters I want to have a look at the contemporary accounts.[4]

Oshana distinguishes three partly naturalistic accounts which are all variants of the split-level-self analysis: the first group she calls "hierarchical theories" and includes, among others, the work of Frankfurt and Dworkin. The second group is labeled "Platonic theories" – here a prominent representative is Gary Watson. The third group is named "historical accounts" – a theory of this kind has been developed, for example, by Christman.

Watson has formulated his theory in opposition to the accounts of Frankfurt and Dworkin confronting their hierarchical theories with counter examples and conceptual difficulties. Christman who for his part criticizes both the Frankfurt-Dworkin account and the platonic account of Watson defends a version of the Split-Level-Self account adding a biographical component to it. Oshana sympathizes with these split-level-self accounts but misses the second naturalizing condition and thus she herself wants to add something which she sees as essential to this account. In the following I give a *short* sketch of the basic ideas of the four versions of the Split-Level-Self account and thereby describe some of the difficulties which each version is confronted with.

The First Step towards Naturalization

A. Classical Hierarchical Theories: Frankfurt and Dworkin

An agent has the capacity to act freely IFF he can do what he wants or desires. Such an agent might nevertheless lack a necessary element for being an autonomous person – i.e., the capacity of having a free will. The central question is, whether an agent has the capacity to will what it wants.

If we label *agents* all those creatures who are able to do what they want or desire, this class will not only include children and other human beings like sex offenders or addicts usually not credited with personal autonomy, but even many animals which nobody would ever regard as free agents. Those creatures, though, who have the capacity to be autonomous, I want to name *autonomous persons*. Because there may be creatures who have a free will but lack the capacity to act freely – for example a completely paraplegic human being – we can define the class of autonomous persons as those who are agents and have free will. And we can say that personal autonomy is composed of the capacities (a) to act freely and (b) to have a free will. Each of these components is necessary and together they are sufficient for personal autonomy. In what follows I will ignore the freedom of action, thus taking it for granted that condition (a) is fulfilled. But one question still remains: How can we analyze the second condition? What does it mean to have a free will?

In his famous paper *Freedom of the will and the concept of a person* Harry G. Frankfurt has given an analysis of the freedom of the will. In a first step he distinguishes between first-order and second-order desires. A statement in the form "I want to X" expresses a first-order desire IFF X refers to actions. And it expresses a second-order desire IFF X refers to first-order desires. A third-order desire is expressed IFF X refers to second-order desires... and so on indefinitely.

Although Frankfurt gives his analysis in the third-person mode of speech I have used the first-person mode, because being autonomous demands that the person ascribes first- and second-order desires to herself. Following on from this Frankfurt defines, in a second step, the will of a person as that desire which is *effective*, which moves an agent "all the way to action" ([8],65).[5] The will of an agent in that sense is not identical with what he *intends* because it is possible that there is a desire which overrules what the agent wants to do (everyone will know examples of this by acquaintance). Thus a statement "I want to X" expresses my will, IFF X refers to the effective desire.

Again Frankfurt adds in a third step the element which – according to him – characterizes personal autonomy or the freedom of the will. I am autonomous, IFF I have a second-order volition, that is a second-order desire I want to be effective, i.e., which I want to be my will. Not every second-order desire is a second-order volition because it is possible that I want to have a second-order desire – for example, if I were to want to have the desire to want to take drugs – while simultaneously not wanting that this second-order desire really becomes effective. All I want is to know in this case is what it's like to have such a desire. If I make a second-order desire my second-order volition I then *identify* myself with the desire which is referred to in the formula. In this way I make this first-order desire *"truly"* ([8],69) my own. Having the capacity to identify with a first order desire by making[6] the corresponding second-order desire my second-order volition is what makes my will free. And if I can make my first-order desires effective I am an autonomous person. According to Frankfurt the freedom of the will can be analyzed as the hierarchical structure of second-order volition with its corresponding first-order desire. The person's autonomy is guaranteed then, because we take the free-agency condition for granted, iff the person can make her second-order volition effective.

Let's look briefly at some of the examples he gives to show the adequacy of his account. An addict who wants to take drugs can act freely IFF he is able to realize this. But his will isn't free. Now one may distinguish different types of addicts if conflicting desires are added to the picture. Addict A has different desires which can't be realized at the same time. But he has no second-order desires. He isn't concerned whether the desires that move him to act are those he *wants* to motivate his action. His action simply realizes his effective desire. Frankfurt calls this type of addict "Wanton". Addict B is an "unwilling addict" ([8], 68). He not only has conflicting desires but he wants himself to be moved by the desire to drink water. But instead he drinks whiskey and so his desire for alcohol was effective. This is something the unwilling addict doesn't like. This second type of addict, the 'unwilling' one, evaluates his own conflicting first-order desires and forms second-order desires. But his will isn't free, because he is unable to transform one of his second-order desires into a second-order volition being effective. He fails to make his elected first-order desire the effective one. Having the second-order volition allows this addict to feel that his will isn't free. He doesn't identify with what he does although his action expresses a desire he surely has. For a person to be autonomous she must endorse her first-order desire by making it truly her own – and that is according to Frankfurt by choosing the corresponding second-order desire to be effective, to be her will. The union of an effective first-order desire and the corresponding second-order volition make up the autonomy of a person, if the second-order volition is a necessary causal condition for the first-order desire's being effective.

Frankfurt has delivered an account of personal autonomy that centers on the hierarchical structure of an individual's *psychology*. Being an autonomous person means having the right internal psychological structure. As well as the obvious difficulties, some important questions remain unanswered[7]:

The first difficulty is that in Frankfurt's account more than two levels of desires or volitions are allowed. But in that case why shouldn't we say that a second-order volition needs a corresponding third-order volition to guarantee autonomy? And why stop at any particular level? Let's name this the *regress problem*.[8]

The second difficulty is closely bound up with the first. If the second-order level is decisive and its autonomy self-sufficient, i.e., is guaranteed without foundation, two further questions then arise: (a) how can these second-order volitions be justified? It seems that here a non-hierarchical alternative account has to be developed, if a simple decisionism is to be avoided. The second question (b) is: why shouldn't the first-order desires be self-sufficient? Why shouldn't we say that a person should correct her second-order volitions in accordance with her first-order desire which manifests itself as being effective? We can label these interconnected problems as the *ab initio problem*.

The third difficulty is caused by the internalism of Frankfurt's account: what do we want to say about the willing addict who fully endorses his wanting a drug by choosing the corresponding second-order volition as truly his own? Let's call this the *formalism problem*: it arises because Frankfurt has given a purely *formal* or *structural* account of autonomy.

The fourth difficulty concerns the internalism per se of Frankfurt's account: we are not born with many of our first- and second-order desires as they are a product of socialization. Take, for example, a woman being educated to obey absolutely her father or her husband. Do we really think she is autonomous if she leads her life this way? One can surely imagine many more examples of this kind. This problem – we may call it the *desire-formation problem* – arises in the above account because of the purely *synchronous* and *individualistic* nature of its analysis.

In contemporary debates many more special problems have been discussed which I cannot go into here. My main aim in the following is simply to outline the common structure of these accounts and to confront it with Hegel's analysis of personal autonomy and the structure of the will as it is developed in his *Elements of the Philosophy of Right*. I'd like now, before I move on, to point out two more basic difficulties in Frankfurt's account which are tied up with his notion of "identification". Frankfurt has used this notion for two reasons: *Identification* signals the capacity of a person to evaluate her own desires, to make herself an object of evaluative considerations. Identifying with a desire by forming a corresponding second-order volition makes this desire truly her own. It is integrated into her self-conception. This is the first reason. The second reason for the use of this notion is, that Frankfurt wanted to solve the regress problem. If a person identifies with a desire there is no room for dissonance on any higher level. But this seems to be a solution only by fiat. We are immediately faced here with a dilemma: either the ab initio problem arises or the process of evaluation collapses into something like an individual "radical choice".[9] This dilemma is the primary difficulty with the notion of identification. The second difficulty is that identification is something a person can and must do intentionally. Here we are facing the problem of whether identification itself is done autonomously. The regress problem or the ab initio problem is back again. We thus also seem to need a separate analysis of the special kind of intentional action called identification. It looks then as if we have just used the very notion of free will – in employing this notion of identification – which we set out to analyze in the first place.

Gerald Dworkin has developed a version of the hierarchical analysis in which the notion of identification is replaced by a capacity clause: for the ascription of autonomy a person's second-order *capacity* is needed in order to evaluate, and if necessary revise, her first-order desires ([4], 15ff.). In this way a person needn't build a second-order volition to act autonomously. It is enough that she has the capacity to do so, if she wants. In my eyes this shift from identification to capacity doesn't really help because we still need a structural analysis of this capacity. And furthermore one can see that a person's using this capacity is just the same process which Frankfurt described as identification. So the problem simply is hidden in a dispositional structure.

B. A Platonic Alternative

In his platonic alternative Gary Watson criticizes the hierarchical accounts of Frankfurt and Dworkin. In his eyes autonomy must be understood as the property of a person being able to act out of reason-based value judgements. According to him Frankfurt and Dworkin don't distinguish properly between different levels of a person's psychology: the non-rational desire system and the rational value system ([24]).[10] In one sense this account is the truly hierarchical account because here the person's psychology is divided in two separate levels. In Frankfurt's and Dworkin's hierarchical account we had only a logical or semantical hierarchy of more complex desires. Watson's classical position seems to avoid the regress-problem because autonomy is bound to the value system without any further clauses. And he surely captures an aspect of autonomy we intuitively have in mind: autonomy and rational evaluation go hand in hand. An autonomous person acts on her rational evaluations and not on her "blind" desires.

Keeping Hegel's critique of Kant in mind, it isn't always the case that, on the one hand, acting according to our rational capacities renders us more autonomous than acting according to our passions. The dualistic account, as Hegel well knew, is in danger of splitting the person and thereby alienating her from her desires. Such an alienation, Hegel claimed since his earliest philosophical writings, cannot be regarded as true autonomy.[11]

On the other hand, Watson's account like Frankfurt's and Dworkin's is also confronted with the other three problems: the ab initio problem, the formalism problem and the desire-formation problem. We need an argument justifying why the rational part should be the bearer of autonomy and why rational evaluations should be regarded as truly autonomous. Without such an argument the ab initio problem still arises. Watson – like Kant – also faces the formalism problem: they try to define autonomy in purely formal or logical terms without giving any material criteria. Hegel has discussed such an approach in his famous critique of Kant's formalism in ethics. In Hegel's view we simply cannot define autonomy without mentioning material conditions for being autonomous. And without including the non-rational part of our psychology into the structure of the will, we are, Hegel maintained, not able to give substance to our notion of autonomy. Finally, Watson also doesn't consider the process of desire-formation by socialization. Like Kant he gives a purely internal and local analysis of autonomy. But as I have said above, evaluations can be formed under conditions which make autonomy impossible. One can imagine examples of educational programmes which form individuals who then act in accordance with their values but are not autonomous because these values are deeply corrupt.

C. The Biographical Completion

It is the desire-formation problem which is the central motive in John Christman's biographical account of autonomy. He wants to include conditions of desire- and value-formation which defeat counter examples of persons who act according to their second-order volitions or value judgements which are manipulated in different ways. According to his model of autonomy a person is autonomous relative to some desire if it is the case that she did not resist the development of this desire when reflecting on this process of development, or she would not have resisted had she been attentive to it. A further condition is that this lack of resistance did not take place (or would not have taken place) under the influence of factors that inhibit self-reflection and the self-reflection involved is (minimally) rational and involves no self-deception ([2], 11).

Without discussing all the details of this we can see that the core idea is the following: not the having of a desire or the actual identification with it is sufficient but the right process of desire formation is decisive for autonomy. Again ignoring the counter factual clauses we can say that personal autonomy needs more than individual psychological capacities. Without the right social and natural conditions it is impossible for an individual to become an autonomous person. Besides the psychological conditions the individual needs, there must be a kind of transparency in its motivating desires – they must be accessible and suitable to its rationality. And the self-reflection condition, too, poses some constraints on the social setting: it must allow individuals to develop a rational self-reflection. An analysis of personal autonomy can't stop at the rational conditions, the natural aspects of the individual must be transparent for the person and they must be integrated into the concept of personal autonomy. And the analysis can't stop at the level of the individual. The social setting has to be considered, too. Autonomy of persons can't be found without the right social surroundings.[12] Neither a purely formal nor a purely internal account can grasp personal autonomy completely.

The Second Step towards Naturalization

In these times of metaphysics-phobia and naturalization the above discussed accounts are attractive because they propose to deliver a naturalistic analysis of personal autonomy. Oshana thinks that these accounts meet the first of her naturalization-conditions: "The conditions given for personal autonomy – that a person's desires and values assume a certain hierarchical structure, or that one's desires cohere with one's values, or that the person has a certain psychological history – are susceptible to methods of explanation employed in the natural sciences." ([12], 91) But, as Oshana claims, none of them is naturalistic because failing to meet her second condition. According to this condition a naturalized account of autonomy cannot be purely internalistic – personal autonomy cannot depend only on the status of a person's psychological states and dispositions. Oshana puts this point as follows: "a person's autonomy depends on the socio-relational environment in which she functions" (ibid.). And over against the biographical account she claims that "the importance of the external realm is not restricted to the effect it has upon a person's desires" (ibid.).

I don't want to deal with the full dimensions of the question of naturalization here. There are to be sure very many different senses of that term and in any case I think Oshana's conditions themselves don't belong to the same conception of naturalization. Whether such central elements of the above accounts such as self-consciousness, identification or rationality really are notions which can be naturalized in line with her conception is a very tricky question and I have my doubts as to its feasibility. That is, I don't agree that the above accounts include a naturalized theory of mind.[13] In regard to this aspect Oshana herself uses a common concept of naturalization but her thesis that the above accounts are naturalistic seems wrong to me. Her second condition for naturalized autonomy says that the use of external properties which are qualified as "objective" is a sign for naturalization. Although I think that her thesis is right regarding the nature of personal autonomy her use of the label "naturalization" is seriously misleading here: the contrast between "internal" and "external" properties does not corrrespond to the contrast between subjective and objective properties. Besides, as Hegel well knew, there are many different senses of "subjective" and "objective" which have to be distinguished carefully, as he himself does in his *Philosophy of Right* ([9], §§ 25 and 26). In regard to the individual the social world is something external, but in regard to Spirit it is internal. Oshana is right in claiming that personal autonomy requires more than an individual psychology. It requires a suitable natural basis and a suitable social world. Thus Oshana is right when she says: "Just as it is unnatural to think of persons as epistemically isolated entities, doubtful as to the reality of anything but the contents of their own minds, so, too, it is unnatural to view autonomy as property that is true of persons in virtue of their inner psychological states, regardless of the circumstances they find themselves in" ([12], 91). But all this can't simply be equated with naturalization. Hegel would agree with Oshana and would claim further that his conception of Spirit and especially his analysis of the structure of the will overcome these deficiencies by developing an account of autonomy of the Spirit which includes personal autonomy as an essential element. In his conception, so Hegel would have claimed, the opposition of internal and external, of subjective and objective is "aufgehoben" and the above discussed problems are eliminated. In what follows I will try to show just this.

II

In the first section of this second part of the paper I will attempt to show how Hegel's account can overcome the dualism of "being internal" and "being external" as well as the subjective – objective divide by distinguishing three levels of analysis. In the second section I will have a look at Hegel's analysis of the person's knowledge of freedom. Taking cognizance of this analysis I will argue that we can solve the above discussed problems by integrating the individualistic perspective – this being the core of the contemporary accounts – into Hegel's richer conception of freedom and autonomy of the will.

The Three Level Analysis of the Will: Overcoming the Internal–External Divide

In his *Elements of the Philosophy of Right* Hegel uses the free will as his starting point. This notion of the will then doesn't mean purposeful behavior in general but purposeful behavior endowed with self-consciousness. This notion of the will is the result of the development of Subjective Spirit and is the basic principle of that part of the system called "Objective Spirit". In starting this way Hegel takes two things for granted: qua will or purposeful behavior in general we have overcome pure causality and are in the domain of teleology which – as the *Science of Logic* has shown – is the truth of causality such that causality is "aufgehoben" in teleological processes. I cannot discuss Hegel's arguments for this claim here.[14] For my present purpose suffice it to say: analyzing free will and autonomy presupposes that causality poses no further problems. As you remember in part One I took the condition for agency as given, saying that an agent could make his mental or psychological states effective. This problem which is central in a theory of action can be set aside when analyzing the concept of autonomy. It is a necessary element for personal autonomy but according to Hegel, we have overcome this problem if we use the notion of the will because this notion implies a kind of teleology.[15] The second point which Hegel takes for granted is that we analyze the self-conscious or thinking will and not those forms of purposeful behavior which can be found both in animals and little children. In what follows I will take the will always to mean the free will endowed with thinking and self-consciousness.[16]

In the introductory paragraphs Hegel marks out three different but in a complex way interwoven levels which we have to analyze when we examine the structure of the will. The first and most basic level is the will's conceptual structure: its "Begriffsnatur" in Hegel's speculative sense of "Begriff". Taken this way the will has to be understood as a *universal* with a special structure which is "logisch" in Hegels special sense of logic. The second level of analysis is the individual's self-consciousness and its knowledge of being free. This self-consciousness delivers the "Begriffsmomente" of the will qua "Vorstellung" ([9], § 4). Analyzing the person's knowledge of her freedom means analyzing the structure of the will in one of its stages of development. The third level of Hegel's analysis is characterized by the thesis which is central for Hegel's whole ethical, social and political philosophy. This thesis claims that ethical, social and political institutions are "Gestaltungen" ([9], § 32) of the free will.

(a) On the first level the free will's "Begriffsnatur" is enfolded. This enfolding includes the will's overcoming the subjective-objective divide. At the outset, though, this "Begriffsnatur" is not "*gesetzt*" for the free will itself, it is, as Hegel puts it, only "*an sich an und für sich freier Wille*" ([9], §§ 34-39).[17]

(b) The second level, encapsulated in the person's "*Vorstellung*" of freedom and autonomy, marks the subjective side of the free will. Being subjective has three different aspects on this second level of analysis ([9], § 25): (i.) the absolute unity of self-consciousness, the "Einzelheit" or individuality of the will, which is expressed in the reference of the indexical "Ich", (ii.) the particular will as having a special propositional content; and (iii.) the one-sided form of the will for which the content belongs to self-consciousness only, such that this content is not yet realized. While the first aspect describes a *universal* instantiated in every self-conscious person, the second aspect *is* the principle of individuation. It necessarily belongs to the will because of its "Begriffsnatur". This first aspect is the so called "spekulative Allgemeinheit", which according to Hegel determines itself, giving itself a special content. The third aspect marks an internal deficiency of the free will on this second level of analysis – i.e., the individual's "Vorstellung" of freedom.

These three aspects characterize the subjective level of the will. The moments of Allgemeinheit (aspect a) and Besonderheit (aspect b) belong together because the will's structure must be "Einzelheit" at all levels. On the subjective level this Einzelheit belongs to the will's *form*, only. This means, as Hegel has shown ([9], §§ 5-16), that the subjective will of an individual is active and moves itself to objectivity, that is, to realize the content of the will.

(c) The third level of Hegel's analysis captures the objective side of the will's structure. The will's being free must become objective because of the will's "Begriffsnatur". This objectivity can be seen, according to Hegel, in the structures of social or political institutions and in ethical life ([9], § 4). These systems of rights are the objective, realized freedom of the will – the Objective Spirit has unfolded his material content by developing objective structures through which the subjective will can realize its freedom. This objective and material side of the will has also three aspects ([9], § 26). The first aspect (i) Hegel names "der schlechthin objektive Wille", that is the will actualized in an ethical, social and political structure which is adequate to its "Begriffsnatur". This aspect marks the *telos* of the will's self-determination and self-explication. The second aspect (ii) Hegel names "objektiver Wille". This historical form of the will lacks self-consciousness. An individual which has no distance to its desires or wants, deficient in what above was analyzed as second-order volitions, is a realization of such a will. Hegel's examples are the will of the child, the will of the slave and of the superstitious, and – somewhat surprisingly – the ethical will. The third aspect (iii) of objectivity is the opposite to the purely formal self-consciousness characterizing the subjectivity of the will: in this sense objectivity means "die Unmittelbarkeit des Daseins", that is, the external existence in space and time and as a natural being. The world in which I have to realize my will as well as my natural aspects as a human being are the complementary material aspects of the will which complete the "Begriffsnatur" which – as I have just explained – is the will's essence on the first level of Hegel's analysis.

Looked at from Hegel's speculative point of view the three aspects of the subjective and the objective sides of the will, that make up the second and the third levels of his analysis, complement each other. In Hegel's eyes the development of a person's autonomy and the historical development of ethical, social and political institutions can be understood as a complex interwoven process encompassing these two developments. The telos of this process then is an ethical, social and political reality by means of which personal autonomy is fully realizable.

The formal or subjective side of the will, which is analyzed on the second level, includes Hegel's analysis of the internal structure of personal autonomy. The material or objective side of the will, which is analyzed on the third level, includes Hegel's analysis of the ethical, social and political institutions as well as the natural aspect of the person's will – its embodiment as a single person. This is the external side of the will. Of course it is Hegel's metaphysical first level of analysis, his theory of "Der Begriff" as it is developed in his *Science of Logic,* which allows him to show that the internal and the external sides of the will cannot be understood in a dualistic fashion but have to be regarded as two aspects of the universal structure of the will. This metaphysical first level allows him to avoid the dualism that can be found in other classical and contemporary approaches. Some of these dualisms are, for example, the opposition of personal autonomy and socialization, the opposition of the cognitive and the volitional side of rationality and the opposition of desires and rational evaluations which itself is one form of the more general opposition of self-consciousness and embodiment.

This interpretation of the structure of free will in terms of his "spekulative Methode" allows Hegel to show how the natural existence as a singular organism and the pure self-consciousness of the "Ich" belong necessarily together. Hegel claims to have shown this in his *Science of Logic*: the absolute mediation ("Vermittlung"), the pure reflection of the "Ich", is initially abstract, that is, an immediacy ("Unmittelbarkeit") and as such it belongs necessarily to the complete structure of the "Begriff" (cf. [14]). Hegel himself then identifies the absolute mediation with the person's knowledge of her freedom in such a way that we find this logical relation there also. Regarded, so to speak, from the inside, in terms of the second level, there is the opposition between pure self-consciousness on the one side, and the person's being a natural being on the other – that is, between the internal and the external. Understood in terms of the first level of analysis, i.e., Hegel's speculative interpretation of the structure of the will, this dualism of the internal free dimension and the external determined dimension which is constitutive for the person can be seen as belonging to the one and unique "Begriffsnatur" of the will regarded as an universal structure. Hegel not only has overcome the dualism on the first- or metaphysical level of analysis he also shows which *function* the dualism has in developing an adequate account of personal autonomy. Overcoming this dualism demands overcoming yet another internal-external dualism: the 'schism' between personal autonomy and ethical life.

As we have seen the contemporary accounts identify the "being internal"–"being external" dualism with the "subjective"–"objective" dualism and they regard this as an antagonistic state of affairs. Hegel disagrees with this view on two grounds: firstly, the distinction between "internal" and "external" cannot be identified with the subjective–objective divide. There are subjective structures – of political or social institutions for example – which are external to the person's autonomy understood as her psychological structure.[18] And there are objective structures – the universal structures of self-consciousness – which are internal to the person's autonomy. Secondly: according to Hegel the determinations "subjective" and "objective" or "internal" and "external" can't simply be regarded as antagonistic. They are "Reflexionsbegriffe". This means that their meaning is constituted by a semantical or – in Hegel's sense – logical relation to each other. It is impossible to define the one without regard to the other. And it is impossible to assume one side of the relation as given and then subsequently to try to deduce the other. In Hegel's view this holds not only for concepts but also for phenomena as he regarded meanings and their logical structure as themselves being the essence of phenomena.

According to Hegel these dualisms have to be understood as *moments* of an underlying speculative unity. The whole phenomenon – in our present context: the freedom of the will – can be understood adequately only, if these dualisms are taken as elements of a complex but unitary structure.

Personal Autonomy as Part of the Will's Structure: Overcoming the Problems of Contemporary Accounts

According to the basic idea of the hierarchical accounts personal autonomy must be analyzed in terms of the logical or semantical structure of a person's psychology. A person's being able to evaluate her own desires which belong to one level on the next higher level and her ability to to identify with such desires on the one hand and her being able to make the desires effective on the other were the key elements in these accounts. These higher-order desires or volitions mark the capacity of the person to distance herself from her lower-order desires. In Frankfurt's and Dworkin's account this capacity was understood as a logical structure only. In Watson's account an ontological dichotomy between the rational and evaluative and the non-rational capacities replaces this logical structure. And along with Christman's account, the other theories also try to analyze personal autonomy with regard to internal psychology only. On top of that, these three approaches all try to give a purely formal account of personal autonomy.

Hegel would have agreed with some of the philosophical theses of these contemporary approaches – but he would also have criticized some of their underlying premises. According to him personal autonomy is a capacity of persons because of their self-consciousness. The notion of identification in various ways central to the above accounts has a theoretical and a practical dimension. In the process of self-determination a person recognizes her true self and evaluates it in one selfsame act. Self-determination then is a cognitive and deliberately evaluative act in uno actu.

In his theory Hegel avoids the dualism of thinking and willing: in his account having a special content, or intentionality, is understood as willing ([9], § 6). And self-conscious willing is a propositional attitude which gives itself a thought content. In this way Hegel bypasses a central problem other accounts are confronted with: the practical and motivational force of rationality is guaranteed by its very own structure – i.e, *intentionality*.

According to Hegel an autonomous person's will is characterized by three aspects:

The *first* is having the first-person mode of thought ([9], § 5) – Hegel identifies this with the "Begriffsmoment der Allgemeinheit". In thinking herself as an "I" a person distinguishes herself from every content her thinking and willing may have. Being intentional this self-consciousness is a kind of willing oneself – and so the person is also willing herself in it. The subjective freedom derives from this capacity of the will to refer to itself in pure self-consciousness and the possibility to choose something different, which is included therein. According to Hegel this freedom must not be regarded as the sole aspect of freedom: isolated from the complete structure of the will this freedom degenerates to a destructive form which Hegel names "negativer Wille"([9], § 5).

The *second* aspect of the free will is that it tends towards self-determination ([9], § 6). Because of the will's "Begriffsnatur" the "Allgemeinheit" of the first aspect must determine itself. On the personal level this means that the person has to give the will a special content. By doing so she identifies with the chosen content and makes it *her* will. In Hegel's account this self-determining activity can't be regarded as a second step in which the freedom of the first step is lost. What is lost according to Hegel is the one-sidedness of the first aspect.

The *third* aspect ([9], § 7) brings the reason for this to light: the will's structure must be analyzed as "Einzelheit", that is, as the unity of the first and second aspect. We can't simply start from the first aspect and try to find criteria within pure self-consciousness alone for true self-determination, nor can we start from the state "being determined" as a natural and socialized being searching for a formal procedure to transform these given contents into a free form. Self-determination of the will has to be conceptualized as the logical interdependence of the first and second aspect which belong together in every person's free will. No person wills her "Ich" purely and without further content. And no person wants merely the content of her will. In wanting something a person always wants *herself* and the content as *her* content.

Hegel warns us not to think of self-determining autonomy as something the will or the "Ich" understood as "vorausgesetztes Subjekt oder Substrat" ([9], § 7) does. The failure involved in the notion of identification as discussed above is just this: the person is taken as given and an attempt is made to look solely for the autonomous mode of self-determination. This model has to be replaced by Hegel's analysis of the will's "Begriffsnatur". If accepted the regress-problem and the ab initio problem wouldn't then arise.

A. *The Regress Problem*

The regress problem emerges because in contemporary accounts the first and the second aspect of the will are kept in isolation. The first aspect, "die Allgemeinheit" of the I, is posited as being constant while the second aspect, "die Bestimmtheit", receives a more and more complex logical structure. But while the content develops in this analysis the will's other moment, the I, doesn't itself develop – its capacity to reflect doesn't change. Interpreted in this way no union can be reached – every mediation fails and we get a structure Hegel has analyzed in the *Science of Logic* as "schlechte Unendlichkeit". The I and its content aren't able to merge in this structure. Of course, in his "Logik des Begriffs" Hegel has developed a model to overcome difficulties of this type. In our present context his solution would be to regard the I and its contents as two dependent moments of the will's underlying structure. The hierarchical accounts correctly analyze the *form* of this underlying structure as it appears to the person's mind in her knowledge of freedom. But this *appearance* of freedom in its 'psychological' form should then be understood as in fact being the appearance of the underlying unity of the will.

B. The Ab Initio Problem

This problem arises for the same reasons. If we take the two aspects in isolation either the first or the second could become the source of autonomy: *either* the capacity to build second-order volitions and to identify with first-order desires *or* the content's logical structure itself would then have to be considered the source of the person's autonomy. But each alternative, taken by itself, is deficient: the person's capacity to identify or build reflective contents cannot generate any contents without falling back into an empty decisionism. And there is no reason to assume that autonomy can be found in the content's logical structure which doesn't itself refer implicitly to the I and its capacities.

According to Hegel we have to regard the will's *complete* structure as the source of autonomy. There is no fixed starting point – no fixed content and no underlying presupposed I as a substratum ([9], § 7). It is the complete self-determining movement of the "Begriff" which alone is the absolute foundation. But this basis is *actuality* and process and not a fixed starting point. Again Hegel would have claimed that Frankfurt or Dworkin have analyzed the *appearance* of this freedom only as it appears to the person's mind in her knowledge of being autonomous and free. In this "Vorstellung" the will's autonomy becomes "für sich" and that means, the person can grasp her being autonomous by allowing contents of the form to be analyzed in such an hierarchical manner. This is an essential moment in the will's development but it isn't the source of autonomy itself. Through our knowledge of having free will the freedom of the will makes itself known. And in this knowledge the structure of the will becomes explicit, but this *becoming explicit* doesn't make it alone the source of autonomy. On the other hand, this becoming explicit *does* belong to the will's self-explication and self-determination. Hegel takes this up in his thesis that an individual's will which lacks this kind of self-consciousness – the "bloß objektiver Wille" – is not an adequate realization of the will's autonomy. Not only the will of the child or of the superstitious man but also the ethical will as Hegel understands the Greek form of ethical life, for example, don't amount to a full realization of the will's structure. This structure not only demands a formal structure of personal autonomy but also an adequate material content the will develops in and through itself. Thus, with the help of Hegel's three-level analysis of the will's structure as discussed above, we can find an account which overcomes the two other problems mentioned above: the formalism problem and the desire-formation problem.

C. The Formalism Problem

Not only Kant, but the contemporary accounts too, face the difficulty of not being able to deliver an adequate account of those contents which are suitable to the autonomy of the will. Hegel's critique of Kantian formalism in ethics and the dualism between the two faculties, rationality and the system of desires, is well known. In an analogous way this critique applies to Watson's dualistic account as well as to the purely subjectivistic and formal accounts discussed above.

According to Hegel the "Begriff" or "Subjektivität" can't be understood as autonomous if it is a purely formal capacity merely appropriating given contents. Besides delineating this basic structure in his theory of Subjective Spirit Hegel also shows that rationality and free will can't exist as separate capacities apart from desires, the senses and activities of all kinds – in other words: rationality and free will have to be embodied in an organism. So the rational and the sensitive parts of a person's psychology must be understood as *aspects* of one unique structure. This explains why desires are transparent to self-consciousness and can be socialized in a reasonable way thus making freedom and autonomy possible. As Hegel shows in the third part of his *Elements of the Philosophy of Right* the basic forms of ethical life are the adequate realization of the will's natural aspect. Ethical life transforms the desires into a reasonable form allowing human beings to be free.

And if we recall the third level of Hegel's analysis with its thesis which claims that social and political institutions are themselves formations of the will we can see that social and political reality isn't external to the person. In fact just the opposite: for the adequate development of autonomy social and political institutions are needed in so far as these are basically of the same structure as the person's autonomy. The relation between the person's autonomy and the political and social world has to be understood as that internal self-determining activity of the will which gives it those contents in which its absolute autonomy can be realized.

D. The Desire Formation Problem

Finally, let's take a quick look at the desire formation problem, for which we may find a solution in Hegel's thesis which claims that the main purpose of social and political institutions is to allow self-conscious persons to lead an autonomous life. According to this insight the person can realize her autonomy only if she recognizes and acknowledges that the social and political – prima facie external – reality has the same basic structure as her own autonomy. So according to Hegel there are three different criteria which qualify desires as suitable for personal autonomy: first, they must be acquired in a social process which itself is part of a political and social life which itself in turn makes the autonomy of persons possible. Second, the person must be able to acknowledge that the social world is something she can identify with. And third – the philosopher's perspective: – it must be shown that the basic structures of the person's autonomy and the social and political institutions can be understood as interdependent moments of the self-determining will, itself understood as a universal structure. Because of the will's absoluteness there is no outside. The ultimate criterion then for the *actuality* of the realized structure of absolute self-determining freedom is that the following is the case: persons can lead their lives autonomously in the full sense of the term only if they identify with the social and political world in which they live.[19] This, though, we would expect to be the case in Hegel's holistic philosophy. But it is only fair to say that this holism contains some possibly dangerous tendencies as well as some open questions, which are particular to it. I would like to close by discussing these briefly in the third and final part of the paper.

III

There is no philosopher whose thinking is more consequently "holistic" than Hegel. The above discussed holism with respect to personal autonomy and the structure of the will is just one aspect of his systematic holism. As we have seen above holism in regard to autonomy and the will is an attractive option though not without consequences. To make things clearer, I will distinguish a number of different levels. For our purposes it is essential to keep the *ontological* and the *ethical* aspects of Hegel's thinking apart. Hegel's ontological holism with regard to the mental has its difficulties, too. But as we can see in the contemporary philosophy of mind, the essence of the mental might best be regarded as externalistic and holistic. Thus given that, Hegel's ontological thesis, which says (i) that an individual's having mental states of propositional self-consciousness presupposes the existence of a social world to which this individual itself belongs; and says (ii) that an individual's having personal autonomy presupposes the existence of a suitable structure of the surrounding social world; is a plausible thesis worth defending.

But, as Tugendhat has tried to show ([23], chapter 13 and 14), isn't there an ethical holism in Hegel's philosophy also? Isn't there a line of thought, which leads to inacceptable ethical consequences where it comes to the determination of the ethical relationship between the individual's freedom and the community's or state's interests? Recalling for a moment the long standing critique of Hegel's political and ethical thought on the one hand and the problems of modern society stemming from the atomism of the individuals on the other, this question becomes accute. Can Hegel give us a lively and convincing model of the relationship between personal autonomy and the social and political world, which is still attractive for us today? Or is his holism an obstacle which makes it impossible to try to find answers to our problems in *his* philosophy?

To answer these questions the problem Tugendhat's critique hints at, has to be refined.[20] Four questions have to be distinguished. The *first* is, whether an ontological holism has necessarily to lead to an ethical holism. Tugendhat has argued that in Hegel's philosophy the ethical holism – stating the priority of the social whole – is founded in his theoretical notions of self-consciousness and truth ([23]). But even if there are some limiting conditions for ethical thought originating from the ontological model there is no strict deduction possible. And, indeed, in Hegel's ontology, the whole is – even on the ontological level – determined as giving the parts autonomy. Hegel's theory of subjectivity, as it is developed in his *Science of Logic*, tries to show that a truly absolute whole cannot exist without giving freedom and autonomy to the parts because it has actuality only in the free interaction of these moments of itself.[21] Thus it is not permissible to argue for the inadequacy of Hegel's ethical theory if taking one's starting point from his ontological holism. And so the *second* question arises: has Hegel in fact really defended a version of the ethical holism which says that the individual's moral or rational choices can be overruled by the imperatives of the social or political system? The answer to this question is: no. But not only that, Hegel also wants to make two important positive points: (i) there is no stable moral choice or moral autonomy without a given and partly accepted social world and (ii) a social or political system cannot adequately analyzed or legitimized philosophically if one starts with autonomous rational individuals and purely non-historical natural laws. That though surely doesn't amount to a subordination. On the other hand the thesis defended by Lübbe-Wolff ([11]), that Hegel's *Elements of the Philosophy of Right* includes all basic individual rights and Hegel has only avoided discussing them under that label out of historical and political expediency, goes too far. Of course most of them are included in what Hegel calls ethical life – as Siep ([19], chapter 12) has shown in detail – because morality is "aufgehoben" and not simply negated. But there are some tendencies in Hegel's political and ethical thought which betray an imbalance in favour of the whole over the individual. – Some of these tendencies are explainable with regard to a number of Hegel's motives which are not themselves essential to his system. In the context of an adequate theory of autonomy these elements can legitimately be neglected.

But we are now confronted with the *third* question: aren't there, as Tugendhat has claimed, some systematical reasons for these tendencies in Hegel's philosophy? Is it really possible to revise these features of his thought without giving up his basic premises? I cannot discuss this difficult question here.[22] All I want to say is that we have to distinguish the different questions carefully. It seems implausible to me that a single feature in Hegel's philosophy can account for those tendencies which today we cannot accept. Maybe teleology is one of the cluster of features, as Siep seems to believe ([17], 294 ff.). Or perhaps particular theological motives, as I suspect. And without being able to argue this point here I would claim that the sources of these tendencies must be seen in some aspects of Hegel's logic. They are not to be found in some, as I see it, lesser features of his philosophical thinking. And so this question basically comes down to the question whether some aspects of Hegel's system can be detached from his *Science of Logic* or whether some aspects of the logic can be eliminated from the rest.

Everyone who knows Hegel's philosophy knows how difficult it is to answer these two distinct questions. In other words – and this is our *fourth* and final question –: do we have an alternative account which solves these problems, the problems Hegel wanted to solve? As far as I can see there is no one theory yet available which itself doesn't face its own problems also. And there are many theories on offer which don't even approximate to the depth of analysis which we find in Hegel's philosophy. Therefore the result must be: as long as we do not have such an alternative theory which allows a more satisfying account we should continue to bear Hegel's *Elements of the Philosophy of Right* in mind as an important theory about personal autonomy and freedom of the will.

Notes

[1] Compare ([16]) and the collections of essays ([1],[5] and [7]). John Martin Fischer's Introduction gives an excellent overview of the main themes of this debate ([5], 9-61).

[2] Cf. my discussion of these topics ([15]).

[3] The same strategy is used in my ([13]).

[4] I will give only a rough overview of these accounts and will ignore the developments some of the theories discussed – especially the theories of Frankfurt, Dworkin or Watson – have made in the meantime.

[5] I ignore here the clauses "will or would move" which Frankfurt adds to this definition. For a discussion of these special problems see Fischer's analysis ([5] and [6], chapter 7).

[6] Here the "control"-condition comes into play (cf. Fischer ([6], chapter 8). Control is, according to Frankfurt, what makes my will free, identification is, what makes me responsible.

[7] The following list of problems (and their names) I have partly taken from Christman ([2]).

[8] In Hegel's *Science of Logic* the general structure of this problem is analyzed as "schlechte Unendlichkeit".

[9] This is Charles Taylor's term, cf. ([20], 290).

[10] Thalberg has critized this as too rationalistic ([22]) and Watson has since agreed in a later paper ([25]).

[11] We do not have to follow here Friedrich Schiller's reading of Kant. In Kant's eyes as long as our desires and passions are in accordance with our rationality and values we don't have to suppress them. Nevertheless according to both the Platonic and the Kantian accounts the real bearer of autonomy is the rational part of our psychology alone.

[12] And because the suitable social setting is a starting condition for personal autonomy the social reality cannot be constructed out of autonomous persons. Using Charles Taylor's illuminating distinctions, made in the context of the liberal-communitarian debate, Hegel is a holist in the ontological sense ([21], 181).

[13] To deny naturalization in this sense doesn't commit me to a dualistic

solution with respect to the body-mind problem.

[14] But compare the helpful analysis of de Vries ([3]).

[15] I have said more about the relation between causality and teleology in my analysis of Hegel's concept of action ([13], 237ff.).

[16] For a more detailed interpretation of this see ([13], chapter 2 and [14]).

[17] This logical determination I have analyzed in detail in ([14]).

[18] With regard to the current debate about the externalism of the mental Hegel could be viewed as a "grandfather" of externalism because of his antirepresentational and social analysis of the mind.

[19] This criterion can be used as a critical standard also: if the philosopher can show that identifying with a given ethical, social and political structure doesn't allow the realization of autonomy in the full sense, this would demonstrate that the given structure is not an adequate realization of the will's freedom.

[20] In what follows my arguments have profited very much from Ludwig Siep's interpretations (cf. [17] 285-294, [18] and [19], chapters 12, 13 and 14.

[21] A more detailed answer is given by Ludwig Siep ([18]).

[22] Sometimes the use of the concept of "organism" in Hegel's political philosophy has been regarded as the source of these tendencies. But as Siep has shown, this isn't the case ([19], chapter 13) with respect to his political theory. Hegel has developed a very differentiated concept of "organism" (cf. the analysis of Wolff [27]) which cannot be reduced to a biological notion.

References

[1] Christman, J. (ed.): *The Inner Citadel*. Oxford 1989.

[2] Christman, J.: "Autonomy and personal history". *Canadian Journal of Philosophy* 21 (1991), pp. 1-24.

[3] deVries, W.A.: "The dialectic of teleology". *Philosophical Topics* 19,2 (1991), pp. 51-70.

[4] Dworkin, G.: *The Theory and Practice of Autonomy*. Cambridge 1988.

[5] Fischer, J.M. (ed.): *Moral Responsibility*. Ithaca 1986.

[6] Fischer, J.M.: *The Metaphysics of Free Will*. Oxford 1994.

[7] Fischer, J.M. & Ravizza, M. (eds.): *Perspectives on Moral Responsibility*. Ithaca 1993.

[8] Frankfurt, H.G.: "Freedom of the Will and the Concept of a Person". In: J. Christman (ed.): *The Inner Citadel*. Oxford 1989, pp. 63-76.

[9] Hegel, G.W.F.: *Grundlinien der Philosophie des Rechts oder Naturrecht und Staatswissenschaft im Grundrisse* (= Werkausgabe Band 7, herausgegeben von E. Moldenhauer & K.M. Michel). Frankfurt a.M. 1970.

[10] Hill, Th.E. Jr.: *Autonomy and Self-Respect.* Cambridge 1991.

[11] Lübbe-Wolff, G.: "Über das Fehlen von Grundrechten in Hegels Rechtsphilosophie". In: H.Ch. Lucas & O. Pöggeler (eds.): *Hegels Rechtsphilosophie im Zusammenhang der europäischen Verfassungsgeschichte.* Stuttgart/Bad Cannstatt 1986, pp.421-466.

[12] Oshana, M.A.L.: "Autonomy naturalized". *Midwest Studies in Philosophy* 19 (1994), pp. 76-94.

[13] Quante, M.: *Hegels Begriff der Handlung.* Stuttgart/Bad Cannstatt 1993.

[14] Quante, M.: "'Die Persönlichkeit des Willens'. Eine Analyse der begriffslogischen Struktur der §§ 34-40 in Hegels Philosophie des Rechts". (in press)

[15] Quante, M.: "Absolutes Denken". *ZphF* 1996 (in press).

[16] Shatz, D.: "Free Will and the Structure of Motivation". *Midwest Studies in Philosophy* 10 (1985), pp. 451-482.

[17] Siep, L.: *Anerkennung als Prinzip der praktischen Philosophie.* Freiburg 1979.

[18] Siep, L.: "Kehraus mit Hegel? Zu Ernst Tugendhats Hegelkritik". *ZphF* 35 (1981), pp. 518-531.

[19] Siep, L.: *Praktische Philosophie im Deutschen Idealismus.* Frankfurt a.M. 1992.

[20] Taylor, Ch.: "Responsibility for self". In: A. Oksenberg Rorty (ed.): *The Identities of Persons.* Berkeley 1976, pp. 281-299.

[21] Taylor, Ch..: "Cross purposes: The Liberal-Communitarian Debate". In: Ch. Taylor: *Philosophical Arguments.* Cambridge 1995, pp.181-203.

[22] Thalberg, I.: "Hierarchical Analyses of Unfree Action". In: J. Christman (ed.): *The Inner Citadel.* Oxford 1989, pp.123-136.

[23] Tugendhat, E.: *Selbstbewußtsein und Selbstbestimmung.* Frankfurt a.M. 1979.

[24] Watson, G.: "Free Agency". In: J. Christman (ed.): *The Inner Citadel.* Oxford 1989, pp. 109-122.

[25] Watson, G.: "Free action and free will". *Mind* 96 (1989), pp. 145-172.

[26] Wolf, S.: *Freedom within Reason.* Oxford 1990.

[27] Wolff, M.: "Hegels staatstheoretischer Organizismus". *Hegel-Studien* 19 (1984), pp. 147-178.

Jussi Kotkavirta

HAPPINESS AND WELFARE IN HEGEL'S PHILOSOPHY OF RIGHT

When Hegel maintains that the task of philosophy is to demonstrate the fundamental identity between what is rational and what is actual,[1] he is summarizing the idea which he exposes in all his work, namely his synthesis between ancient and modern philosophy. For Hegel, as for the ancients, philosophy studies being from a rational point of view, asking how the actual forms of things correspond to their concept or idea.[2] At the same time Hegel thinks that modern philosophy, especially the critical philosophies of Kant and Fichte, have opened new and important options for this rational point of view by reflecting on the general structures of subjectivity. Hegel's practical philosophy should also be read as an original synthesis of especially Aristotelian motives and certain modern ideas based on the notion of free will. One theme in which this Hegelian combination of ancient and modern elements may be unveiled concerns happiness and welfare as they are discussed in his *Elements of the Philosophy of Right.* In the following, I will try to explicate this combination and also comment on

Hegel's possible significance for the contemporary debates concerning questions of good life.

Generally, for Hegel happiness (*Glückseligkeit*) and welfare (*Wohl*) belong to the normative apparatus of practical philosophy, notably because of their central roles within the intentionality of our everyday life. Hegel thinks that it is the task of practical philosophy to give a conceptual presentation of the various legal, moral and political phenomena in a way which captures our practical orientation also towards happiness and welfare, situating this orientation properly within the totality of our intentionalities. Hegel follows, I think, principally Aristotle in conceiving the normativity of various practical phenomena from the viewpoint of the intentionality of life itself, and not from any separate idea of the good, or from pleasure in the hedonistic sense, or from the idea of maintenance of the whole in the Stoic sense. On the other hand, he thinks that the Aristotelian approach as such is not adequate when we study the actuality or rationality of modern ethical and political life. Instead of the classical discourse of *eudaimonia* one must, in the modern times, conceptualize practical life by starting from the notion of will as various forms of the autonomy of will, i.e. following the Kantian and Fichtean theories of practical rationality. For Hegel, too, the highest human good is not happiness as such but freedom. But for him happiness and welfare have their prominent and constitutive roles in the actualization of freedom in human life.

In the following I examine first the systematic structure of Hegel's *Elements of the Philosophy of Right* and especially the roles of the notions of happiness and welfare in it. I will do this briefly and avoid going too deep into the dark waters. It seems to me, however, that Allen Wood in his excellent discussion on the notions of happiness and welfare loses something essential when he overlooks Hegel's metaphysics of will-structures altogether.[3] Secondly, I will discuss in more detail Hegel's chapter on morality, especially those parts in which happiness and welfare are treated. Finally, I will study briefly the role played by happiness and welfare in Hegel's discussion of the civil society and the state. My overall aim is to clarify our picture of the specific Hegelian synthesis of the broadly Aristotelian and Kantian elements – elements which as such are for Hegel abstract and one-sided approaches to the intentional and normative structures of modern life.

The Roles of Happiness and Welfare in Hegel's Systematic Procedure

Hegel says that the subject-matter of his *Elements of the Philosophy of Right (PR)*[4] is "the idea of right – the concept of right and its actualization" (§ 1). For Hegel, concepts must have their actuality or existence (*Dasein*), and vice versa. A concept of right alone would be an empty abstraction, and likewise a study of legal phenomena in their existence, without their concept, deals merely with contingent, unsubstantial appearances. The concept and its existence are "two aspects of the same thing, separate and united, like soul and body" (§ 1, A.). The idea of right is freedom, which then must be recognized "in its concept and in the concepts existence" (§ 1, A.). *PR*'s aim is to elaborate the concept and existence of the free will as a totality of shapes of the right. It is a dialectical presentation, proceeding from abstract to concrete, from simple to complex, of the various institutional forms of free will. Hegel intends to show how the will externalizes itself into various forms of its existence and how it simultaneously creates more and more complicated conceptual relations to itself. In these self-relations the consciousness of freedom develops, and Hegel's systematic idea is to study modern society as the totality of forms of this consciousness, i.e. as spirit.[5]

Hegel himself formulates the unity of the two aspects as follows: "The will which has being in and for itself is *truly infinite*, because its object (*Gegenstand*) is itself, and therefore not something which it sees as *other* or as a *limitation*; on the contrary, it has merely returned into itself in its object. Furthermore, it is not just a possibility, predisposition, or *capacity* (*potentia*), but the *infinite in actuality (infinitum actu)*, because the concept's existence (*Da-*

sein) or objective (gegenständliche) externality is inwardness it-self" (§ 22). Thus, as *truly infinite* the will constitutes structures of self-relation in which finite and infinite, particular will and universal will produce mediations instead of mere oppositions. That which originally does not belong to the will is no more treated merely as the other, as something alien, but is taken into the self-determinations of the existing will, i.e. into the sphere of right. As we shall see, this is exactly what occurs with happiness and well-being, too, when Hegel thematizes them as essential moments of action.

The will is, except truly, also *actually infinite*. Thus it is no mere possibility, or capacity (*potentia*), but the actualization of a capacity. In the same way in which we, according to Aristotle, can-not have potentiality without actuality, the notion of freedom and its various forms of *Dasein* belong inherently together in Hegel's thought. The free will can be comprehended only as it externalizes itself in the various form of action, as it actualizes itself. A trans-cendental deduction of the unity of concept and *Dasein*, of the ca-pacity and its actualization, would necessarily remain abstract. Because the will's autonomy for Hegel is not a pure self-relation, in the sense in which it is for Kant, but evolves in the action itself, happiness and well-being are also moments in its constitution. Thus, the will begins its self-determination with regard to natural inclina-tions, drives, desires, which then supply content to the will. This is made clear in the introduction to *PR*.

In the beginning, the will is free only in its concept, in itself, and it will gain freedom for itself only gradually as it makes itself into its object (§ 10). The will may have as its content both external objects as well as internal images, but at this initial stage it has no means or criteria with which to organize its content coherently. The will is immediate, or natural, which means that the content appears for it in the form of immediate impulses, desires, and inclinations in the sense that the will is actually determined by this content. Hegel contends, however, – very much unlike Kant – that this content is something implicitly rational, though it has not yet found its rational form (§ 11). Natural impulses, inclinations and emotions belong to human free-dom; in fact, they constitute its essential content. Before they are made mine, however, i.e. as long as they are not integrated into my individuality, they exist as mere desires. As such each of them is something unlimited, indeterminate and directed to all kinds of objects and forms of satisfaction (§ 12).

The idea of happiness, then, is intended to bring order into these natural drives. Hegel introduces this idea roughly as follows. First the will posits itself as an individual will. As a pure form it distances itself from the content, situates itself above the content and reflects this in order to make choices between various drives. At this immediate stage, the contingency of its content makes the will itself arbitrary (§ 15), so that the repressed content returns. The result is that the will is all the more dependent on the content in its attempts to deliberate and make choices. It has yet no means for justifying its decisions. There is no rational coherence in its choices (§ 16). This contradiction between content and form appears, then, as "a *dialectic* of drives and inclinations", in which every drive exists against others demanding satisfaction. The will cannot make but contingent choices between them, as it calculates and maximizes its satisfaction (§ 17). Similarly its judgements about the impulses are purely arbitrary: now it maintains that they are naturally good, then that man is naturally bad, without a rational means of settling such disputes.

The only way out of this bad circle, according to Hegel, is to make the impulses part of "the rational system of will's determination; to grasp them thus in terms of the concept is the content of the science of right" (§ 19). Here the idea of happiness has a central function. Its task is to bring some kind of generality, coherence and shape into the derangement of desires and drives. Hegel defines happiness here as "the sum of total satisfaction", equating it with subjective welfare (§ 20). Here he is not so far from Aristotle, for whom eudaimonia unveils itself for each subject in his practical activities and is thus not to be defined from an external, third person perspective – neither as a universal idea nor as a neutral calculus.[6]

"In happiness thought already has some power over the natural force of the drives, for it is not content with the instantaneous, but requires a whole of happiness" (§ 20, A.). Hegel maintains that the subjective universality inherent in the idea of happiness, and in the corresponding idea of education, is still abstract and undeveloped. Thus, when the will begins to reflect on the impulses and drives, estimating and comparing them against each other, calculating their cost and future benefits, it "confers *formal universality* upon this material" (§ 20). Because this whole, the universal, is merely an *ideal* of happiness as universal pleasure, the "universal end is itself particular, so that no true unity of content and form is yet present within it" (§20, A.). Such a unity presupposes not only will, but thought and knowledge as well. Hegel emphasizes throughout his work the connection of thought and will. Thus he maintains also here that because universality is present merely as pleasure, subjectivity and feeling in the idea of happiness, a unity of form and content presupposes thinking. For only in thought and knowledge may the immediacy and particularity of natural will be superseded (*aufheben*) into something universal (§ 21).

These are no more than preliminary definitions of happiness and welfare in the introduction of *PR*. Hegel develops his idea of free will in three stages. As a concept it is presented in universality, particularity and singularity. As a relation between concept and its *Dasein* it is presented firstly in terms of logic of being, as abstract immediacy, and secondly in terms of logic of essence, as reflection into itself, and finally in terms of logic of notion, as the unity and truth of the preceeding moments. These are the three main parts of *PR*. At the first stage, i.e. in abstract right, happiness and welfare are not discussed because they do not exist as such for the legal personhood. As long as a person recognizes himself only in the external objects as his property, there is no room for reflection on happiness.

At the second stage, i.e. morality, sensuous externality of the I and its internal freedom separate from one another; distancing from the external things the I begins to become aware of its own particularity. It starts to become *for itself.* "This reflection of the will into itself and its identity for itself, as opposed to its being-in-itself and immediacy and the determinacies which develop within the latter, determines the *person* as a *subject*" (§ 105). For this subject, then, as we shall see, universality presents itself either as a duty or as a universal good. The tension between universal as concept and particular as *Dasein* is built into Hegel's treatment of the moral will, and it is the context where also happiness and welfare are principally discussed. At the third stage of ethical life, finally, the two preceeding moments are presented as mediated and united. "The embodiment of freedom which has (a) first of all immediate as right, is (b) characterized in the reflection of the self-consciousness as good. (c) The third stage, originating here, in its transition from (b) to ethical life, as the truth of the good is therefore the truth both of subjectivity and right" (§ 141, A.). At this last stage also happiness and welfare are discussed as embedded in the ethical life of family, civil society and state.

The Morality of Happiness and Welfare

In morality the immediate relation of the legal person to external objects breaks and the I begins to reflect on itself as a subject. Thus a shift in perspective takes place. Hegel presents here his view on the nature of the moral will and its roles in human action.[7] Its mode of *Dasein* is moral subjectivity which reflects on itself. In the reflection there opens a new difference between universal and particular, but Hegel argues that conditions for their higher unity begin to emerge as well. The moral standpoint "takes shape of the *right of the subjective will.* In accordance with this right, the will can *recognize* something or be something only in so far as that thing is *its own,* and in so far as the will is present to itself in it as subjectivity" (§ 107). Thus the will, which is for itself, recognizes something only in so far as it wills this and takes it to be good for itself. At the same time, however, a moral duty or a more universal good presents itself as a demand to the I. Here Hegel wants to demonstrate how a legal person transforms himself into a moral subject who is not only for itself but may accomplish a moral duty or a universal good as well. In the chapter on morality these two demands are recognized and related to each other within reflection – but nothing more. Unlike Kant, Hegel thinks that only after superseding morality into ethical life can we think properly of their rational unity. Only then can we see the general lines along which modern subjectivity accomplishes the univeral good in accordance with the idea of right.

Hegel's position in respect to the Kantin distinction between morality and legality is a complex one. Ethical life as a whole is meant to provide a mediation between them, but Hegel also discusses in his chapter on morality topics which belong to Kantian legality. Thus the whole chapter on "Intention and welfare" (*Absicht und Wohl*), in which happiness is treated, has no equivalent in Kantian morality. This is so, generally speaking, because Hegel situates moral will into human action itself, and not into motives preceding action like Kant. Hegel, too, distinguishes the will as a rational capacity from its various empirical determinants, but he does not do this absolutely. His intention is to reflect on the way in which the various components and determinants of the will measure each other in action, as subjective and objective, particular and universal. In Hegel's opinion, we may study knowledge only in its work, and similarly we may study the will only in its work, i.e. in action. Action for Hegel is "the expression of the will as *subjective*" (§ 113). The chapter on morality, then, has three sections in which Hegel wants to indicate how the contradiction between internal and external, which emerges when the subject intends to act, is resolved from a moral point of view.

In the first section, entitled "Purpose and responsibility" (§ 115–118), Hegel characterizes the intentionality of action and its moral components. An action presupposes external objects with their complex environment, for it aims to carry out a change in them. It is important for Hegel to emphasize that the will is responsible for changes only "in so far as the abstract predicate 'mine' attaches to the existence so altered" (§ 115). Among the many consequences only those belong to the action which are intended by the will, which fall under its purpose. "I can be made *accountable* for the deed only if *my will was responsible* for it – *the right of knowledge*", Hegel remarks (§ 117). Thus the morality of an action is also a matter of its intended consequences. Hegel criticizes both Kant who neglects the consequences, as well as such consequentalism which does not recognize "the right for knowledge": "In so far as the consequences are the proper and *immanent* shape of the action, they manifest only its nature and are nothing other than the action itself; (...) But conversely, the consequences also include external interventions and contingent additions which have nothing to do with the nature of the action itself"(§ 118, A.). Hegel connects the intended consequences with the subjective principle of action, i.e. maxim, whose morality, then, is under examination. For Kant, this examination concerns merely subjective motives, ultimately the relation of the will to itself. For Hegel, however, this kind of moral autonomy is basically an empty ideal which distorts the picture of our responsibility for actions.

In the second section, bearing the tittle "Intention and welfare" (§ 119–128), Hegel then connects happiness to action, arguing that both the Kantian ethics as well as the eudaimonistics doctrines of virtue are one-sided, abstract views on the matter. He situates happiness and well-being into a complex structure of the will, in which the particular and the universal first seem to distance more and more from one another. The will, which is now characterized through its intention (*Absicht)*, is no more arbitrary as it was when it considered its purposes and consequences, because now it seeks to gain a general picture of its situation. Thus the will studies its various purposes and their connections with both the actor's own and more general needs, wishes and interests.

As an external event, as *Dasein*, an action is a complex set of connections which may be analyzed and explained differently in causal terms. Hegel asserts that its truth as an individual act, however, is a universal one (§ 119). This is so because the purpose, which is central to the event as an action, "as emanating from the *thinking* agent, contains not just the individual unit, but essentially that *universal aspect* already referred to – the *intention*" (§ 119). Hegel thus makes a distinction between purpose and intention. While the purpose in the first place contains the actor's own perspective to the action, the intention contains its universal aspect. Hegel suggests a re-interpretation of the Kantian maxim by bringing the intention into the center of moral considerations. He demands that the actor has "the *right of intention*", i.e. the right to know the universal quality of the action and to will it subjectively (§ 120). The other side of the matter is that she has "the right of the *objectivity* of the action", i.e. the right to know and will her action "*as a thinking agent*" (§ 120).

The intention thus connects the universal aspect to the action. This by no means overrules the actor's subjective purposes. Hegel puts much weight on this point: "But the subject, as reflected into itself and hence as a particular entity in relation to the particularity of the objective realm, has its own particular content in its end, and this is the soul and determinant of the action. The fact that this moment of the *particularity* of agent is contained and implemented in the action constitutes *subjective freedom* in its more concrete determination, i.e. the *right* of the *subject* to find its *satisfaction* in the action" (§ 121). For this reason the action has subjective value for the actor and is in her interest (§ 122). Here we thus have, first, an actor who is realizing her purposes and intentions, and secondly the subjective content for these ends, i.e. "needs, inclination, passions, opinions, fancies". "The satisfaction of this content is welfare or happiness, both in its particular determinations and in its universal aspect – the end of finitude in general", as Hegel defines it (§ 123). He adds further that unlike in the introduction to the book, "the will here is not as it is in its immediacy; instead, this content, belonging as it does to the will reflected into itself, is raised to a *universal* end, namely of *welfare* or happiness". Such a universal meaning of welfare and happiness emerges here as one reflects on the morality of action.

Thus, it turns out that for Hegel happiness, or subjective welfare, is essential to the morality of an action. Hegel does not mean that happiness were higher than freedom, or the sole content of it. His point is that happiness and freedom, the demands of life and reason, are fundamentally in accordance with each other: "There is nothing degrading about being alive, and we do not have the alternative of existing in a higher spirituality. It is only by raising what is present and given to a self-creating process that the higher sphere of the good is attained (although this distinction does not imply that the two aspects are incompatible)" (§ 123, A.). Thus, subjective welfare is among the essential ends of an action, its "living core". One should neither overrule it by some other universal end nor elevate it to the only end. These latter views, criticized by Hegel as one-sided abstractions, lead to the dangerous implication that "because subjective satisfaction is present (as it is *always* when a task is completed), it constitutes the agent's *essential intention* to which the objective end merely was a *means*" (§ 124). This would detach the subjective satisfaction completely from other ends. If morality then is related positively or negatively to it, a subject acting morally is not responsible for the objective aspects of her activities. This is exactly what Hegel opposes.

Very much like Aristotle Hegel maintains that both the ends of life as well as those of reason are present in our action. In action, properly conceived, they actually go together: "What the subject *is, is the series of his actions*. If these are a series of worthless productions, then the subjectivity of volition is likewise worthless; and conversely, if the series of the individual deeds are of a substantial nature, then so also is his inner will" (§ 124). Hegel is, on the other hand, very conscious of the fact that in modern times subjective and objective values by no means always meet each other – that the views which he is criticizing do reflect essential tendencies in these times. There is only a thin consensus about the substantial value of an action, and the views about happiness or subjective welfare vary individually more and more. This is something which cannot and shouldn't be opposed as such. "The right of the subject's *particularity* to find satisfaction, or – to put it differently – the right of subjective freedom, is the pivotal and focal point in the difference between *antiquity* and the *modern* age", he maintains (§ 124). In modern times the search for happiness – or for authenticity, in terms suggested by Charles Taylor – is realized in most varying individual and cultural forms. It would, in Hegel's opinion, be a fatal mistake to defend morality as something which contradicts this freedom – as "the injunction: 'Do with repugnance what duty commands'" (§ 124 R.).

Like Aristotle before and Nietzsche after him[8], Hegel emphasizes that if morality is defined as opposition to life, it is not conceived properly. On the level of morality alone, however, one cannot cancel (*aufheben*) this opposition, perceive the unity of morality and life. Morality, in the sense Hegel thinks of it, opens a space for the subject to reflect on the different purposes and intentions connected to the action. The solutions to the problems, opened by such a reflection, of how to reconcile the tensions between individual and universal welfare are practical and concrete, however, and depend on the institutional context. Within the moral reflection individual and universal are present as demands, or rights, which the subject may recognize, but there are yet no guarantees that they meet each other.

Finally, in the last section – entittled "The Good and the Conscience" (§ 129–141) – Hegel defines, first, the idea of good in a specific sense. This may be read as a parallel to Kant's idea of the highest good. For Hegel, an idea is not merely an ideal; it has its actuality as well. The idea of good collects all the determinations developed so far, and at the same time it formulates the universal end of action which up to this point has been present merely as an abstract demand. Hegel says that "(The good is) *realized freedom, the absolute and ultimate end of the world*" (§ 129). Here Hegel again makes a strategic reinterpretation of Kant.

Kant would never have maintained that "the good is the absolute and ultimate end of the world". For him the *Endzweck* is the "highest good", defined as the unity of morality and happiness, and understood as a regulative idea which directs our action but may never be realized. For him the good, or the idea of good, is not the *Endzweck* because the good is determined through the moral law and cannot thus be its end. Hegel, too, emphasizes that the two moments, welfare and freedom, coincide in the good: "Within this idea, welfare has no validity for itself as the existence (*Dasein*) of the individual and particular will, but only as *universal* welfare and essentially as *universal in itself*, i.e. in accordance with freedom; welfare is not good without right. Similarly, right is not the good without welfare (*Fiat justitia* should not be *pereat mundus*" as its consequence)" (§ 130). However, Hegel makes a very conscious return to the tradition, criticized by Kant, when he connects morality to the good.

Here his idea of the good resembles especially the Aristotelian eudaimonia, the highest end among all possible ends of human action and life. It is not the Kantian unity of morality and happiness or subjective satisfaction in the maxim preceeding the action, but a more substantial unity of the universal and particular will and their content, i.e. welfare, *in the action*. "The good is the truth of the particular will, but the will is only what it commits itself to; it is not by nature good, but can become what it is only by its own efforts", Hegel writes, insisting that the good must be known and specified by the will and be for itself as conscience (§ 131). Hegel stresses that our responsibility for our actions presupposes that we have the right to know the relevant determinations that make our actions good or evil. He obviously is thinking of Kant when he remarks: "Consequently, the assertion that human beings cannot know (*erkennen*) the truth, but have only to do with appearances, or that thought is harmful to the good will, and other similar notions (*Vostellungen*), deprive the spirit both of intellectual and of ethical worth and dignity" (§ 132).

So far Hegel has indicated how the subject relates the particular and the universal with each other within the intentionality of her action. Happiness and welfare have their roles in this intentionality, which ultimately is directed towards the good. When Hegel in the third part of his book discusses the rational structure of modern ethical life, he wants to show in more detail how subjective will realizes itself in action together with an ethical and political community, in which the good may be present.

The Limits of Happiness and Welfare

In the third and most extensive part of *PR* Hegel elaborates the fundamentals of modern ethical life. The preceeding moments of the universal good and the particular will are presented here in their living unity, as embedded in the structures of family, civil society and state. Individual happiness and welfare also have certain roles and functions within the modern ethical totality: "The right of individuals to their *particularity* is likewise contained in ethical substantiality, for particularity is the mode of outward appearance in which ethical exists" (§ 154). The locus where Hegel studies the development, refinement and satisfaction of particular ends is his theory of civil society. In his view, civil society, as distinguished from family and state, is a social and economic sphere or space in which modern individuals are given free hands to find satisfaction for their particular ends.

Hegel's strategy here is twofold. On the one hand he defends maximal individual freedom to realize oneself within "the system on needs". On the other hand he insists that this system is no more than a subsystem within the substantial ethical and political community, i.e. the state. Civil society has its own rationality and limits between family and state. In modern civil society, Hegel writes, "the selfish end in its actualization, conditioned in this way by universality, establishes a system of all-round interdependence, so that the subsistence (*Subsistenz*) and welfare of the individual *(des Einzelnen)* and his rightful existence *(Dasein)* are interwoven with, and grounded on, the subsistence, welfare, and rights of all, and have actuality and security only in this context" (§ 183). This system of mutual dependence, the system of needs, opens for the particularity a historically unique space to find satisfaction in varying ways. But, and this the problem for Hegel, this search of happiness is fundamentally contingent. It continues to create new ends, desires and needs, without limit or purpose. Hegel says that here particularity ultimately "destroys itself and its substantial concept in the act of enjoyment". "In these opposites and their complexity, civil society affords a spectacle of extravagance and misery as well as of the physical and ethical corruption common to both" (§ 185).

For Hegel it is apparent that happiness in the modern sense means in the first place subjective satisfaction. This is likewise most essential in the modern ideas of individual freedom. However, although labour and consumption are the driving forces of modern society, Hegel maintains that they cannot be conceived as its *Endzweck* alone. After elaborating on his double perspective on the civil society, Hegel goes on to introduce his means for limiting the system of needs, which with its contingencies also threatens individual happiness. The problem of poverty is a hard one for Hegel, and he attempts to solve it by introducing the police and the corporation as a kind of nightwatchman, representing the universal within the civil society. "Through the administration of justice, *infringements* of property or personality are annulled. But the right *which is actually present in particularity* means not only that contingencies which interfere with this or that end should be *cancelled (aufgehoben)* and that *undisturbed security* of *persons* and *property* should be guaranteed, but also that the livelihood and welfare of individuals should be secured" (§ 230).

The police is a public authority which not only prevents crimes but also creates infrastructure needed for economic activities, regulates markets, protects consumers, promotes public health and education, and prevents enemployment (see § 231–249). This authority, thus, protects individual welfare against the contingencies of civil society and guarantees that each member of society has access to the material prerequisites of participation in society.[9] By corporations Hegel understands private associations recognized by the state as corporate bodies (see § 250–256). "The corporation has the right, under the supervision of the public authority (*Macht*), to look after its own interests within it enclosed sphere, to admit members (...), to protect its members against particular contingencies, and to educate others so as to make them eligible for membership. In short, it has the right to assume the role of a *second* family for its members, a role which must remain more indeterminate in the case of civil society in general (...)" (§ 252). Thus, a corporation promotes the welfare of its members and, as a kind of "second family", supports their group and individual identities.[10]

Finally in Hegel's discussion of the modern state, the significance of happiness and welfare is constantly emphasized. He writes e.g. that: "The principle of modern states has enormous strength and depth because it allows the principle of subjectivity to attain fulfilment in the *self-sufficient extreme* of personal particularity, while at the same time *bringing it back to substantial unity* and so preserving this unity in the principle of subjectivity itself" (§ 260). Taken together, thus, happiness and welfare do have an outstanding role in Hegel's theory of right. There is scarcely another philosophy of right in which these notions would be given a corresponding weight. Hegel's view of happiness and welfare is indeed a modern one. He conceives them in terms of the subjective satisfaction of individual desires, needs and inclinations. He allows this satisfaction its maximal freedom. At the same time Hegel insists, however, that the contingencies of civil society should be administered to the extent that this system of needs does not threaten itself, families or the state. Civil society is pivotal in modern life, but it is by no means the whole picture of it; analogously, happiness and welfare are central in our action and life, but they are by no means all of it.

Hegel is a defender of a welfare state in the sense that welfare is essential to the idea of society and that the public authority should guarantee a certain stability and justice in the distribution of welfare. However, he opposes state perfectionism in the sense that the state could dictate what the subjective welfare of the individual is or should be, or that state would somehow be founded on the ideas of happiness. Hegel agrees with Kant, who thinks that happiness in modern times is so indeterminate and individually varying that one can found neither ethics nor political theory on it. Freedom preceeds individual happiness and welfare. But the meaning of this liberal principle is different in Hegel's *Philosophy of Right* from its meaning in Kant's practical philosophy. For Kant, happiness and welfare are conditional in the sense that a subject must first and foremost be worthy of them, i.e. be capable of forming and testing his maxims before considering these natural ends. For Hegel happiness and welfare, intended by the subject, are essential for his self-actualization and freedom, within the whole of his good. This Hegelian good, "the unmoved end itself" (§ 258), is after all perhaps not so far from that for which Aristotle used the term *eudaimonia* and for which it is so difficult to find a proper translation.

Notes

[1] Preface to *Elements of the Philosophy of Right.*

[2] Cf. e.g. Hegel, *Enzyklopädie der philosophischen Wissenschaften*, § 24.

[3] See Allen Wood 1990, *Hegel's Ethical Thought.* Cambridge University Press, Ch. 3.

[4] *The Elements of the Philosophy of Right.* Transl,. H.B. Nisbet. Ed. Allen Wood. Cambridge University Press 1991.

[5] This systematic idea is not as apparent in *PR* as it is especially in *Jenaer Reaphilosophie* of 1805/06. See Hegel, *Gesammelte Werke, Bd. 8.* Meiner 1976.

[6] Wood (1990) emphasizes the rift between ancient and modern views on happiness and presents Hegel as a modern author, whose conception is subjective in the sense that the content of happiness is determined by individual desires and that this content may vary from individual to individual. All this is different from the objectivistic and fundamentally egoistic classical view. It seems to me, however, that Wood defines the terms all too unequivocally and makes the contrast too strong.

[7] See Michael Quante, *Hegels Begriff der Handlung.* Fromman-Holzboog 1993.

[8] On this connection between Aristotle and Nietzsche see Walter Kaufman, *Nietzsche. Philosopher, Psychologist, and Antichrist.* Princeton University Press 1974, Ch. 12, and Hans Ruin, Det måttlösas mått – Nietzsche, Aristoteles och etikens pånyttfödelse. In Michael Carleheden, Margareta Bertilsson (red.), *Det goda livet. Om resessanssen för en borttappad diciplin.* Symposion 1995, p. 153–172.

[9] Cf. Michael Hardimon, *Hegel's Social Philosophy. The Project of Reconciliation.* Cambridge University Press 1994, p. 195–197.

[10] See Hardimon, *op. cit.,* p. 197–205.

Markku Mäki

MODERN SOCIETY IN ROUSSEAU AND HEGEL

M arxian materialism might be defined without essential loss of meaning as the following thesis: the social structures of the modern monetary economy[1] and its division of labour give or at least tend to give their own structural characteristics to almost every kind of social relationship or cultural feature in modern society[2], however "distant" from them. This thesis is by no means a Marxian intervention. The section on the system of needs in Hegel's *Elements of the Philosophy of Right* (*PR*) presents an instance of it. Hegel's account is both extensive and dense. He drew to that effect heavily on the classical political economy (*PR* § 189, Remark).

Rousseau did not provide anything comparable to Hegel's account in one piece. Nonetheless, he agreed with the thesis and had a rather systematic vision of its ramifications. Contrary to appearances, Rousseau's view of the modern world is *not* in the last instance totally critical. Rather, it was deeply, sometimes despairingly double-edged. In this essay I will compare Rousseau's and Hegel's remarkably analogous views about the problem of modern society. For a *problem* it indeed is for both. I also try to contextualize their most conspicuous differences concerning that problem.

Having completed his theology studies in Tübingen, Hegel spent around 1795 some three years as a tutor at Bern. At that time his view of the modern world and its political problem was very close to that presented by Rousseau in his *Essay on Inequality* and *Social Contract*. Omitting minor issues, one can say that they differed at one point only, i.e. over the question of civil religion. That question was first of all a *political* question for both. Civil religion should unite the people culturally, as a foil to its political and civic union.

Rousseau considered the problem of civil religion in the last section of Social Contract. He discarded Christianity as a possible civil religion because of its otherworldliness. More importantly, he almost despaired in general of the possiblity to unite modern enlightened faith and seremonial appearance of any kind, because the latter seemed to be against the spirit of self-determination. He nevertheless constructed a "religion of citizen" with few and very general doctrines. It has an air of unconvincing formality and calls only public confession.

For Hegel at least the *problem* was to find a religion which could support the common subjectivity of a people (*Volkgeist*). As Rousseau – and mostly for analogous reasons – he came to disqualify Christianity. But the solution would be necessarily a "mythology reason", a concurrence of the reason and the myth on the one hand and of the enlightened elite and the masses on the other hand[3].

Hegel thought that a civil religion could be neither a construct without roots in the fantasy of the people nor some antiquated myth, say Greek or old-German. In the end, the only possibility left was a reformation of Christianity. There is in his extensive and mainly very critical studies on Christianity during those years no hint about any concrete form of such a reformation. In general one can say that Hegel stressed more the cultural side while Rousseau's approach was more immediately political.

The Concept of Freedom

The concept of freedom is no doubt the most important common ground for Rousseau and Hegel. Hegel regarded Rousseau's concept of freedom as the most important predecessor to his own. The concept of free will developed in his the introduction to *PR* is indeed of the same type as Rousseau's, e.g. *autonomical*. "Autonomical" means here[4] not only "independent" but "being able to legislate for oneself", both personally (for one's desires) and politically. It means not only that one must legislate every important law one must obey, but that there should be laws defining for a people its genius and for an individual its personality.

Of course, the form of autonomy only gives the necessary condition for someone to be free. A prisoner might on the one hand be called free in the sense of maintaining his integrity even in such a situation, but on the other hand also unfree in the sense of not being able to realize his personality. An important intuition behind the autonomical concept of freedom is that one should not call free anything which is not a person.

One can very well desire without being a person. Thus "being unhindered in the course of one's desire" cannot be any overall characterization of freedom in this view. We can see here an analogy to Kant's theory of the highest good. In the same way as morality legitimizes happiness in it, we can say here that to be unhindered in the course of one's desire is a positive or completing ingredient of one's freedom, provided that it is legitimized by one's own law of personality. But note that thinkers like Rousseau, Kant and Hegel did not accept as a law of personality anything incompatible with morality.[5] Indeed, Kant's categorical imperative is the paradigmatic case of autonomical freedom.

Most essential is that the concept of autonomical freedom was for both Rousseau and Hegel the *fundamental principle of political legitimacy*. Both Rousseau and Hegel use the same concretization of autonomical freedom, (the predominance of) *general will*, for the legitimacy of a state (*P* III, 361; *PR* § 258). Concerns of need, expediency, self-preservation or welfare are of importance but secondary nature. In this Rousseau and Hegel differ from the mainstream of modern political thinking. Kant's concept of the highest good again gives an analogy: freedom must be thought as a precondition for permissible welfare (happiness). For both Rousseau and Hegel, right is always a modification of freedom. This is instructively expressed in their concepts of property. For both it is primarily not a concept of self-preservation, livelihood or welfare, but one of the foothold of freedom (*P* III, 262ff; *PR* §§ 45, 46).

The System of Needs in Modern Society

There was very much fundamental agreement between Rousseau and Hegel concerning the system of needs.[6] There are two principles in Hegel's theory of it that express its division of labour: 1) *concrete personality* and 2) *form of universality* (*PR* § 182). The former is the right of everyone to futher just one's own interests. Rousseau's well-known critique of modern society employs concepts like *amour propre* (vanity, egoistic feelings, insatiable passions, etc.), *relativity* (identity not through oneself but the others) and *egocentrism* (immorality, desire of domination over the others). Much of their content is mediated by the principle of concrete personality. At the same time, the intensive mutual dependency of people characterizing modern society[7] on the basis of its division of labour is their very important backround factor, as it is that of Hegel's other principle, form of universality. Hegel's criticism of the modern society through the principle of concrete personality is no less sharp than Rousseau's.

The form of universality is for Hegel that side of modern culture which counters and binds the otherwise destroying forces of concrete personality. It rests on the fundamental necessity for people to orient themselves towards socially valid ways of work and communication in the intensive dependences of the monetary economy. It is the ground of the principle of equal reciprocity in modern society. For the first time in history each individual is in principle equally competent in possessing and trading commodities, including one's labour power. The most concrete expression of the form of universality is the principle of *recognition (Anerkanntsein)*, which is nothing less than the overall characteristic of the social institutions of modern society, manifested in myriads of contractual acts (promises included) based on it (*PR* §§ 192, 193).

Certainly Rousseau saw the modern world as the world of intense mutual dependency or of relativity, as he put it in slightly different terms. It might not be as obvious that Rousseau would have had any equivalent to the principles of the form of universality and recognition. However, the principle of recognition or equal reciprocity plays an important role at certain epocal points in *Émile*. It is there highly ambiguous a principle. Émile has to meet it as a rudimentary but absolutely necessary principle of sociability years before he is apt to learn anything about ethical life in general[8]. Nevertheless, Émile meets in and through it the facticity of relativity (*P* IV, 334) which threatens to destroy *naturality*[9], the criterional quality of Émile's upbringing (*P* IV, 247).

This ambiguity is but one expression of the general ambiguity of civil society which intensifies in several dimensions both good and evil possibilities. As Rousseau said in *Émile*: "We have entered the moral world; the gate is open for vice" (*P* IV, 334). Indeed, for him as for Kant there is no virtue without a struggle against temptation, and the harder the struggle, the more respectable the virtue. Hegel had a lot of trust in the ability of the form of universality to curb the destructive tendencies of the concrete personality, while Rousseau mostly regarded the very expressions of it as corruptive. This is partly because it seemed to express the mutual dependence of people, partly because of its homogenizing effects.

Certainly, homogenization is for Rousseau as it is for Hegel part of civilization. But for Rousseau civilization was ambiguous in itself. On the one hand it eliminates personal differences which might otherwise be resistant to corruption, on the other hand civilized behaviour is often a treacherous illusion or a cover of scheeming. Hegel knew that kind of critique well, even accepted it to a certain extent, but he does not be pursue that aspect in *PR*.[10]

In the first paragraph of this essay it was claimed that the mate-

rialistic thesis was shared by Rousseau and Hegel. This is manifested in their sharing an insight into a close connection between
modern subjectivity and modern society. Their thinking is grounded
on an idea according to which the modern division of labour does not
give its subjects only certain cultural qualities and arts but a certain
general tendency and structure of subjectivity. For both, antropology
was manifestly not some set of characteristics common to people of
all ages and whereabouts. It was rather tied to a unique *history*,
ending in modern society and articulated in retrospection from it.
This means that for Rousseau e.g. the antropological perspective
was not *basically* from the state of nature to modernity, but the
other way round.

The most characteristic *negative* feature of the modern subject
for Rousseau (and partly for Hegel as well) has already been dealt
with above. The *positive* characteristics of the modern subject for
both are 1) the conception of equal and reciprocal rights, 2) the
conception of moral autonomy. The genesis of all the subjective characteristics is comprehensible only on the ground of the genesis of
the structural ones.

The positive feature in question is conspicuously manifest in *PR*.
As a matter of fact, its first two main sections (abstract right, morality) analyze those features, and one of the main implications of its
famous dialectical method obtains readily in its third and last main
section: subjective principles in question presuppose the modern institutional basis (ethical life). Furthermore, it is easy to see that the
modern institutions have as their central *new* material basis in the
system of needs.

That might not be so clear in Rousseau because in his treat-
ments the negative evaluation of modern society tends to hide this
aspect. But it is not too veiled either. As evidence for this one could
quote Book I, Chapter 8 of *Social Contract*, where Rousseau in
fact tries to sell to the skeptical or hesitating mind the legitimacy of
society in general and a fortiori that of modern society. Many passages in *Émile* could also be quoted to that effect.

The Inevitability of a Political Solution

On the basis of the analysis in section II it is to be stressed that both saw modern society as a *society of ambiguity*. More precisely, they saw it as having a tendency to ruin the noble possibilities implicit in modern subjectivity. This state of affairs brings them both to seek a political solution to the dilemma. For Rousseau as for Hegel, civil society is not able to solve its problems without political intervention. Rousseau was in general quite sceptical about any possible solution. But even Hegel had to admit that the *intrinsic* resources of civil society would be insufficient. Thus the form of universality alone is unable to keep the destructive tendencies of the concrete person in check.

In order to avoid the methodological complexities of *PR*, I shall restrict myself only to the relevant material problems, e.g. to its discussions of poverty and polarization (these being each other's mutual causes). Now, that problem cannot be in Hegel's eyes only one problem among others, but rather *the* problem of the modern society. For Hegel thinks that the problem be on the one hand a structural problem, and poverty therefore an inherent tendency in the system of needs. On the other hand it has as its effect the exclusion of its victims from normal societal goods (*PR*, §§ 241-244). That means in effect exclusion from citizenship and rights, e.g. from freedom. But freedom that belongs to everyone is the very precondition of political legitimacy.

Of the means to fight poverty the most important ones presuppose the intervention of the state. At present we could call the strategy Hegel projects for the state a social security policy. It consisted, for instance, of price control, public employment, etc. These means are necessary but not sufficient, even when taken together. For instance, public work results in a surplus of commodities when compared with the solvent demand. "It hence becomes apparent that despite an excess of wealth, civil society is not rich enough, i.e. its own resources are insufficient to check poverty and the creation of a penurious rabble." As a matter of fact, "the civil society" could be replaced here by "the state" (*PR*, 245).

Rousseau finds the same problem of polarity of wealth as dangerous for freedom, though not in exactly the same way. According to him, equality did not by far mean the same amount of wealth to everyone. It meant only that there should not be anyone so rich as to be able to buy another and anyone so poor that he would have to sell himself (*P* III, 391ff). The important accompanying idea was that wealth, especially money, can be used more easily than any other means to acquire other goods, for instance power and domination (*P* III, 189). The good (legitimate) state must therefore restrict the possibilities of acquiring excessive wealth.

Differences between Rousseau and Hegel

So far I have confined myself to issues about which Rousseau and Hegel were mainly in agreement. I now try to say something about their most important differences. Of course, we must take into account that in some aspects the development was rapid in those days; therefore, the almost sixty years Hegel was younger than Rousseau changed Europe a lot.

Sometime around the year 1800 Hegel remarked that the importance of property has grown too mighty for us (*HW* 1, 333). This implied a fundamental point of departure from Rousseau's position. Rousseau thought that the self-sufficency of the modern subjectivity, the main mentality resource of a person against corruption, cannot be preserved despite any kind of politics of any state, if the monetary economy progresses beyond a certain point. Because in that case the polarity of wealth is inevitable. Money and wage labour should not be allowed more scope than it has in the marginals of farm economy on a familiary basis (*P* III, 267ff). Hegel's remark simply points out that the monetary economy will defy all such restrictions.

So, if there is to be any self-sufficiency at all, it has to be found through struggling and overcoming the tensions of the opposite tendency at its height and through strengthening oneself in the flames of the struggle. The remark to *PR* § 185 (Knox translation with a small amendment) says: "Some of these ancient states were built on the patriarchal and religious principle, others on the principle of ethical order which was more explicitly intellectual – in either case they rested on primitive and unsophisticated intuition. Hence they could not withstand the disruption of this state of mind when self-consciousness was infinitely reflected to itself; when this reflection began to emerge, they succumbed to it – because the simple principle underlying them lacked the truly infinite power to be found only in that unity which allows both sides of the antithesis of reason to develop themselves separately in all their strength and which has so overcome the antithesis, therefore maintains itself in it and integrates it in itself."

This kind of insight was understandably not possible for Rousseau. By contrast, it was a fundamental aspect of Hegel's system. On such a principle belonging to the modernity he in fact constructed his entire system with the concept of absolute spirit and its genesis from antiquity to the present time as a world-history. Therefore one can say that Hegel's remark about the monetary economy becoming an invincible fate already is a certain beginning of his road towards a mature system.

Rousseau's conception of history was not a world-history in the same sense as Hegel's. Of course, the story of his essay on inequality is as such a linear story. But that does not make it a world-history in a Hegelian sense. As far as I can see, there seems to be three eras in it: the era of hunters and of nomads and the agrarian era. Therefore he still had to address his own age to the agrarian era, many thousands of years old, as old as private property or the state. He probably did not regard the modern world to be on the threshold of a new era, industrial or some other kind. Rather, he might have expected the corruption of the western countries to continue with the development of the monetary economy and perhaps to lead them towards some kind of general regression or dissolution. There is, however, no evidence to suggest that he thought that these developments would necessarily become very dramatic.

Rousseau saw and analyzed very sharply many features – both corruptive and inalienable – of modern society. He did not see its positive and negative tendencies as inseparably connected, although he regarded them as being connected in the genesis of modern society. In other words, he did not expect the restriction of the monetary economy to entail any cultural loss. Rather, he thought that corruption might be inevitable, at least in the bigger countries.[11]

According to Hegel, the positive and negative features of modern society were inseparable. Thus he had to give up any idea in the effect of restricting the overall development of the monetary economy. But that did not make him support a liberal economy. Quite the contrary, he saw it as inevitable that the state should intervene as strongly as necessary in a struggle against the "contingencies" of the economy people were subjected to and the essentially destructive tendencies of the system of needs.

Notes

[1] Of course, Marx would have used the word "capitalistic" here. From our point of view this is inessential.

[2] "Modern society" is here a name for society which Hegel and Marx called "bürgerliche Gesellschaft" and for which Adam Ferguson first coined the expression "civil society". One should note that the German word "Bürger" means both the citizen and the bourgeois. The system of need of civil society is based on a developed monetary economy which could also be called "capitalistic". The question is how well one can ascribe the concept to Rousseau in the same meaning as, for instance, to Hegel. I believe that its essential themes and contours can be read in Rousseaus's *Essay on Inequality* and *Social Contract*. But I also believe that for him it had not such a clear-cut world-historical meaning as it had for Hegel and Marx. For them it gives, as a matter of fact, the very point of view of grasping world-history. See section IV of this essay.

[3] The famous s.c. oldest system program of German idealism states this standpoint fittingly (*HW* 1, 235). The authorship of this text is open to controversy. I do not want to put forth any opinion thereupon.

[4] I do not try to propose any general norm for the usage of the term "autonomy". The etymology of it is, however, strongly suggestive of the usage of the text which is tighter than the ordinary one.

[5] Why could they, for instance, not admit the possibility of a person

adopting consistently "the law of evil"? The negative answer goes back to Socrates and Platon: for them the evil is only disorder of passions beyond the control of reason, which must be thought of as a faculty of universality not confined to instrumental thinking (to the service of passions).

[6] This is Hegel's term but is quite apt to describe Rousseau's views as well. It should not be taken to refer to any compact one-piece treatment of that theme. But the conception Rousseau must have had in order to present his critique of modern society is bound to be rich and even consistent to some extent.

[7] The egocentrism and the mutual dependency collide with each other in the competitive nature of the system of needs. According to Rousseau, that collision is an enormous source of corruption, because fundamentally it makes people on the one hand competitors, even enemies of each other, and on the other hand compels them to persuade each other to co-operation or bargain which should be advantageous to each party. That makes them wear false masks in their communication and is the main root of the insincerity penetrating modern society in general (*P* III, 202ff).

[8] Rousseau was worried about any learning (of words, of anything) which Émile could not really understand from his own experience. At the beginning of childhood that meant taking into account only his immediate needs and their satisfaction. With more experince, the principle of utility should lead the understanding. Only when sexual maturity was close did the reasoning of ethical life become both necessary and possible. In that period of maturing to self-consciousness and responsibility, there should be also the important point of reflection or of majority: *Émile* is made to understand the whole process of education with its ends, methods and and manipulations. Nothing should be held back (*P* IV, 639, 641).

[9] In *Émile*, naturality means self-sufficiency (autarchy). It has very little to do with the presocial and prehistorical natural condition Rousseau discussed in his essay oninequality. The only possible interpretation for the phrase "Return to the nature!" compatible with what Rousseau said (the phrase itself can be found nowhere in his texts) is "Return to the state of autarchy!" (*P* IV, 305).

[10] This critique rather has its say in *Phenomenology of Spirit*, especially in its section "Der sich entfremdete Geist. Die Bildung", (*HW* 3, 359ff). In Miller's translation: "Self-alienated spirit. Culture." (*PS*, 294ff). In *PR*, the homogenization presents a highly positive moment in civilization. In an addition (from notes taken at Hegel's lectures and edited by Gans 1833) it reads: "By educated men, we may prima facie understand those who

without the obtrusion of personal idiosyncracy can do what others do – Thus the education rubs the edges of particular characteristics until a man conducts himself in accordance with the nature of the thing. Genuine originality which produces the real thing, demands genuine education, while bastard originality adopts eccentrities which only enter the heads of the uneducated" (Knox, 268). Or: "The fact that I must direct my conduct by reference to others introduces here the form of universality. It is from others that I acquire the means of satisfaction and I must accordingly accept their views. – To this extent everything private becomes something social. In dress fashions and hours of meals, there are certain conventions which we have to accept because in these things it is not worth the trouble to insist on displaying one's own discernment, The wisest thing here is to do as others do" (Knox, 269). There is some disagreement about the worth of these additions as source material. When the point in them is as clear as above, doubts seem misplaced. But of course, this material is in general unfit to contribute to cases of hermeneutical twists and delicacies.

[11] In *Social Contract* he suggested one people in Europe capable of (legitimate) legislation, i.e. the Corsicans (*P* III, 391). And only a few years later Rousseau really sketched a constitution for Corsica at the request of a Corsican nobleman, Matteo Buttafoco (*P* III, CCII). This sketch adopts the norms for a legitimate state presented in *Social Contract* in an amazingly literal manner. The agriculture was stressed and the monetary economy restricted to a bare minimum (*P* III, 904ff).

References

HW   1-20 Hegel, *Werke 1-20*. Frankfurt a.M., 1986.

PI-IV Rousseau, *Œuvres complétes I-IV*. Éditions Gallimard, 1964.

PS   *Hegel's Phenomenology of Spirit* (transl. A.V. Miller). Oxford University Press, 1977.

PR   *Hegel's Philosophy of Right* (transl. T.M. Knox). Clarendon Press, 1952.

Ossi Martikainen

The Principle of Subjectivity and Sittlichkeit in Hegel's Philosophy of Right

In paragraph 260 of *Elements of the Philosophy of Right* (*PR*), which opens the discourse of constitutional law (*Das innere Staatsreht*), Hegel collects his thoughts concerning the two sides of ethical life: subjectivity and substantial unity. This is also the first paragraph where the term 'principle of subjectivity' is explicitly used, although there are allusions to it throughout the whole work. My aim here is to consider and systematize the meaning and complementary dimensions of the principle of subjectivity, which I regard as a key to understanding Hegel's views of ethical subjectivity and its relation to objectivity, as well as of the relationship between the state and individual freedom. These problems have been widely studied among Hegel-scholars. However, one can also recognize a certain Hegelian line of argument in the recent critical discussion on Kantian-type moral and political theories. Some forms of communitarian critique of liberalism set an example of this. Thus, my interest in this paper is not only in the explication of Hegel's thought. Towards the end of my discussion, I will also be trying to consider if, and how, it would be feasible to relate Hegel's thought to the current controversies in practical philosophy. I begin, however, by returning to Hegel's discussion in paragraph 260 of *PR*.

The Principle of Subjectivity

At the beginning of paragraph 260 Hegel defines notions of the state and concrete freedom. The latter consists in a process in which

> "personal individuality and its particular interests should reach their full *development* and gain *recognition of their right* for itself (within the system of the family and of civil society), and also that they should, on the one hand, *pass over* of their own accord into the interest of the universal, and on the other, knowingly and willingly acknowledge this universal interest even as their own *substantial spirit*, and *actively pursue it* as their *ultimate end*."[1]

Consequently, neither the particular nor the universal can exist without the other. Thus, individuals in the modern state cannot be conceived solely as private persons. While furthering their own ends, they are at the same time promoting, either unconsciously or consciously, the universal. This essence of modern states is summarized at the end of the paragraph:

> "The principle of modern states has enormous strength and depth because it allows the principle of subjectivity to attain fulfilment in the *self-sufficient extreme* of personal particularity, while at the same time *bringing it back to substantial unity* and so preserving this unity in the principle of subjectivity itself."

It may be useful to single out some of the essential points in Hegel's summary and to explicate the different and complementary dimensions of the principle of subjectivity he puts forward. I begin by considering its practical dimension within certain relations of ethical life [*Sittlichkeit*] set forth in *PR*.

Individuality, Particular Interest, and the Universal

In the development of *Sittlichkeit*, there are two spheres providing the basis for the release of personal individuality and its particular interests: the family and civil society. First, the family forms the basic independent economic unit and thus a sphere for private property. Second, it provides its members with the sphere for immediate feeling of love and unity. It may appear somewhat odd that Hegel regards the family as a sphere of particularization. In the case of the family, particularization means its differentiation from earlier modes of *Stamm* or associations of families, as well as independence from the *Häuser* which the members of new families come from. This independence is a right of the family, which makes it a kind of person[2] in relation to other families. The way and scope in which the head of a family is active in civil society, as well as the corresponding wealth and social position of the family, essentially differ from the opportunities provided by the feudal world of pregiven and limited choices. However, Hegel emphasizes the inherent moment of unity in the family. We could say that as an ethical institution, the family has an aspect of particularization. For its members, however, it has an aspect of substantial unity as well. This latter aspect, which is based on the immediate feeling of unity and the possibility to become recognized as a member of the family, reflects a general process characteristic of all ethical intuitions.[3]

In civil society, the particular interests of individuals constitute the basis of the 'system of needs' (*das System der Bedürfnisse*), a system of self-seeking individuals who strive for the satisfaction of their subjective needs. In this respect everyone is his own end. The particularization that takes place in civil society not only shapes needs, but restructures social positions as well. To exist as an individual, one must enter into determined particularity (*bestimmte Besonderheit, PR* § 207). This requires the individual's decision to limit himself to one of the particular spheres of need, which further demands a freely willed devotion to a specific profession.[4] This also means the possibility to attain a position in an estate (*Stand*).

As a member of an estate, the individual attains recognition for his subjective skills and is able to lead a life characteristic of his estate. In this way he becomes *somebody,* recognized as holding a certain social position. Here the term 'recognition' plays a double role. On the one hand, recognition is given to one's personal, subjective skills. On the other hand, one is recognized *generally* as a member of civil society. The task of this double recognition is given to corporations representing different professions. Here again, as in the case of the family, the moment of universality enters the scene together with the possibility of particularization. In the family this happens in the immediate feeling of love and unity. In civil society this process of bringing particularity back to universality takes place both i) unconsciously and ii) with knowledge and will.

i) In the system of needs we can see the Hegelian version of the invisible hand at work. The satisfaction of needs is, ultimately, not a private matter. First of all, the desired objects are products of the work of others, while the system of markets through which these objects are mediated adds a second aspect of intersubjective dependence and multiplication of needs to this sphere, which at first seemed to be only a matter of private welfare.[5]

ii) The *conscious* devotion of the subject to a particular sphere of needs, and thus to a specific estate and corporation, plays an important mediating role between civil society and the universal interest of the state. Furthermore, the mechanisms of mediation and recognition realize an important aspect of the freedom of subjectivity *within* the sphere of civil society, and thus not only because of their function of genuine political mediation. This aspect can be conceived as an expression and demand of Hegelian positive freedom. The freedom of association (of establishing corporations) is one of the crucial aspects of freedom in modern states. As Steven B. Smith puts it, "...these intermediary bodies prevent either excessive centralization from the state above or excessive atomization from the market below."[6] Another aspect of positive subjective freedom is the right of members to get economic support from the corporation. In both cases, subjective freedom is not conceived negatively, as the lack of hindrance, but positively, as a right to self-expression and partaking of sentimental as well as material goods.[7] Without going further into details, we can see the broad outline of the practical side of particularization and of its return to the universal. The starting point of all ethical formations is a free decision of subjective will. Through the mediations of recognition and membership in the family and corporation, the ethical rights and duties of the individual are rooted in his own willing activity; therefore, instead of constituting a hindrance to his freedom, they serve as the material conditions of its realization.

We have now made an overview of the practical dimensions of the principle of subjectivity, of its release, and of the process in which the particular is brought back to the universal and harnessed to the service of further ends, which override the particular standpoint of the individual without violating his freedom. If we do not want to take Hegel's views as mere opinions or demands among others, we should ask for the foundation for the principle of subjectivity.

The Historical and Systematic Foundation of the Principle of Subjectivity

In paragraph 260 of *PR*, Hegel argues that the principle of subjectivity is an essential feature of modern states. In the states of classical antiquity, only the moment of universality was present, while particularity had not yet been released. Hegel takes this distinction up frequently in the course of his exposition. Contrasting his views with those in Plato's *Republic*, Hegel notes that Plato could not take into account the modern characteristics of particularity, namely private property, family, and the subject freely choosing his profession and position in an estate (*PR* § 186). In the *Preface*, Hegel argues that the modern principle of subjectivity is the feature which Plato tried to suppress by recourse to the external forms of *Sittlichkeit* of his own time. It should be understood that although Hegel often contrasted his own views with those in Plato's *Republic,* he did not consider Plato's views mistaken as such. On the contrary, Hegel thought that Plato had been highly sensitive to the ethical conventions of his time.

For Hegel, the reason to examine Plato's theory is that it provides an opportunity to show that the principles of the states and societal forms of antiquity differ from those of modernity. From the viewpoint of Hegel's philosophy of history we can see history as a process of developing freedom, which in the modern world has reached its final stage, the freedom of each individual human being. Plato could see the birth of subjective freedom only in the 'ratiocination' of the Sophists. For this principle to become recognized and part of the objective reality of ethical institutions required the long history of Christian religion, its culture of inner life, and the Reformation as a new expression of this 'obstinate' subjectivity.

The above-mentioned difference between modernity and preceding historical stages cannot be philosophically explained in terms of historical or descriptive comparison. For Hegel, the principle of subjectivity is not just one feature which happens to emerge in the development of social forms[8]. Rather, the becoming of the modern world should be seen as a slow, but ever progressing actualization of this principle. Therefore, we have to explicate the systematic core of this concept, not just its appearances in the stages of development of ethical life.

In the *Preface* to *PR*, Hegel presents the most compact and eloquent formula for what I take to be the further meaning of the principle of subjectivity:

"It is a great obstinacy, the kind of obstinacy, which does honour to human beings, that they are unwilling to acknowledge in their attitudes (*Gesinnung*) anything which has not been justified by thought – and this obstinacy is the characteristic property of the modern age, as well as being the distinctive principle of Protestantism. What Luther inaugurated as faith in feeling and in the testimony of the spirit is the same thing that the spirit, at a more mature stage of its development, endeavours to grasp in the *concept* so as to free itself in the present and thus find itself therein." (*PR*, p. 22)

In this formula the Hegelian foundation of modernity – the autonomy of reason – has been thought up to its final consequence: to give up all authorities and dogmas for the freedom of thought. From Hegel's *Phenomenology of Spirit* we know the negative way of showing the inevitability of free thought. In the course of *Phenomenology*, such forms of consciousness that assume something to be the ultimate criteria for truth or experience are shown to be inherently contradictory. They have to assume more than they claim in order to present their claim. What, then, is Hegel's positive alternative to those criticized forms of consciousness which rest on some irreducible foundation, i.e. a foundation which cannot be justified by anything beyond itself?

A fairly common interpretation of Hegel's alternative is to argue that his conceptions of absolute knowledge and of the self-actualization of absolute subjectivity constitute a kind of natural or historical theology. In the course of history, individual consciousness and knowledge as well as the objective laws and duties of human communities will begin to correspond to the rationality of the absolute world-plan.[9] This way of reading gives us a static, 'closed' view of Hegel's philosophy, and one which the philosopher himself expressly rejects.[10] The principle of subjectivity, 'obstinacy which does honour to human beings', as it works in the context of Hegel's philosophy of right, cannot be conceived as affirming the social, historical or any other given criteria for the legitimation of right.

Hegel's solution to the problem of inherently contradictory forms of consciousness is his dialectical method. His dialectics should not be understood as confronting one existing alternative with another, nor as a development of those alternatives to an alleged synthesis which would finally progress to the synthesis of absolute spirit. The thesis and antithesis in Hegel's dialectics belong to the realm of the *Idea*, in other words, to the domain of thought and objectivity.[11]

The main point of Hegel's theory is that right (*Recht*) is the existence (*Dasein*) of free will. The system of right realizes free will, and nothing that fails to express the existence of free will can claim to be a right. That *PR* has the idea of right as its object reflects two important things for the modern philosophical understanding of right. First, what is right cannot be derived from some ahistorical or immutable source, i.e. from *lex naturalis*, law of nature. Second, any existing system of right must be open to criticism according to its relation to the idea of right.[12] The beginning of the realization of the idea of right is identical with that of individual free will. In paragraphs 5 to 7 of *PR*, free will is conceived as a subjective will, which has in itself the moments of universality (§ 5) and particularity (§ 6), together forming the individuality (§ 7) of the will.

As the basis of right, this side of subjectivity cannot represent a total and comprehensive view of the will. If it could, the concept of right based on free will would collapse into aporias of *volonté des tous*, which in the absence of unanimity lead either to the authorization of the veto of each individual or to the repression of those minorities that do not will this or that particular law. Hegel's concept of free will acknowledges the system of rights only as a totality of this system. The subjective and objective sides of will (§§ 25–26 of *PR*) are thus not distinct and external to each other. We can say that as a totality of individual will and its objective formations, the system of right is freedom that has freedom as its object. As Hegel puts this in § 28 of *PR*: "The activity of will consists in cancelling [*aufzuheben*] the contradiction between subjectivity and objectivity and in translating its ends from subjective determination into an objective one, while at the same time remaining *with itself* in this objectivity."

In *PR*, the objectification of subjective will into institutions takes the following basic structure: First the individual will has to give itself an external existence. This happens in the form of property and those relations of right which belong to it, discussed in the section entitled *Abstract right*. The next relation-to-self of the subjective will is its own inner reflection about the justifiability of its external actions, discussed in the chapter on morality. Finally, free will is the objective reality of the laws and institutions of *Sittlichkeit*. Now, the systematic dimension of the principle of subjectivity can be conceived as a subjectivity which realizes its own free will as a subject of right. The spheres of right, in which a subjective will stands in a relationship to other wills, are nothing but its own formations. This is meant by the statement of § 147 in *PR*:

"On the other hand, they [ethical powers, OM] are not something *alien* to the subject. On the contrary, the subject bears *spiritual witness* to them as to *its own essence*, in which it has its *self-awareness* (*Selbstgefühl*) and lives as in its element which is not distinct from itself – a relationship which is immediate and closer to identity than even (a relationship of) *faith* or *trust*."

Furthermore, the subjects of modern ethical life are endowed with the possibility to reflect on themselves as legal persons or moral subjects. They are not restricted to the objectivity of ethical life and its institutions and laws.[13] This is because the final stage of ethical life is a result of the formation of subjective will and its objectification. The ethical order is not an order realizing the will of a god-like absolute subject. The ethical order of institutions, laws and customs has its historical basis. But these are valid not because of their sheer facticity, but because they are products of the unfolding of free will – not of a collective 'macro subject', but of the will's relations to itself and to other individual wills.

At the beginning of this paper I took up some practical dimensions of the principle of subjectivity in its connections to the institutions of ethical life. Now there is something to be added to that characterization. If we do not regard ethical subjectivity as an aspect which is confronted to objectivity, but instead see the objective side as formed by the subjective will returning into itself, we can single out some other practical meanings and realizations of the principle of subjectivity. These are generally of two types. One is those institutions and practices whose legitimacy can be measured against the principle of subjectivity, because we can see them as expressions of free will. The other is those institutions which we can see as reflecting the principle of subjectivity. However, the estimation of this second type of institutions can be said to be beyond the reach of individual self-knowledge and thus of individual free will. I will consider some aspects and examples of the first type in more detail.

To illustrate what I mean by the second type, I give only one example, Hegel's theory of monarchy. Hegel's justification of monarchy clearly reflects the principle of subjectivity. The monarch has a rather restricted role in the government of the state. It could even be said that his power is literally reduced to the 'dotting of the i'.[14] Thus, the position of the monarch reflects the principle of subjectivity both symbolically, as the individual head of the state, and concretely, as a natural person, or an individual will. However coherent this view is with the subjectivity characteristic of the modern age, we can see that it is not necessary to accept Hegel's theory of monarchy. I do not mean that we may ignore such parts of Hegel's philosophy of right that do not fit in with the more democratic intuitions of today. What I regard as essential here is that in some questions Hegel is not consistent enough or is 'too consistent' *vis-à-vis* the principle that right and certain institutions are realizations of free will. Instead of discussing the problems of Hegel's theory of government or monarchy as such, I would like to consider briefly the problems of the first type and try to find out whether Hegel's philosophical foundation of right is tenable.

This set of problems entails views which could be taken seriously in contemporary practical philosophy. Let me just mention two of them: (i) the individuality of will; (ii) the subjectivity or individuality of institutions.

(i) Each stage in the system of rights is founded on the individual character of the will. The individual will is not restricted by the objectivity of institutions, but has the ability to maintain a critical distance to them and question their legitimacy. This critical distance must also be maintained by the subject toward his own actions and principles. Hegel expresses the same demand in the *Preface*: 'the obstinacy... not to acknowledge anything which has not been justified by thought'. For him, it is clear that in the modern world it is impossible to have so coherent, unquestionable and in fact unreflected views. I think that some communitarians today underestimate these demands of the individuality of modern life or the problematic nature of our practices.

Hegel's social philosophy has been taken as a paradigm by some communitarians. It is true that Hegel worried about the same things as most communitarian thinkers: the atomizing effects and increas-

114

ing individualization of the market economy as well as the socially atomizing effects of the contractual views in political theory. But it is equally true and important to emphasize that Hegel's cure to these problems is neither a return to the substantial unity of premodern life nor the dissolution of society into incommensurable subcultures. Solutions like these fail to do justice both to rational thought and to free individual will.

(ii) The different stages of right as realizations of free will include forms of subjectivity and individuality that are in complex relations with each other. Because of their common grounding in free will, the different formations and spheres of right can collide. "But a collision also contains this further moment: it imposes a limitation whereby one right is subordinated to another; only the right of the world spirit is absolute in an unlimited sense." (*PR*, § 30)

The Hegelian foundation of right in the existence of free will makes it possible to connect these two aspects. The fact that the different spheres of right may collide in a commensurable fashion can be explained on the basis of the common ground of subjective and objective freedom. This means that within the system of rights in a modern state, the individual may have, and in fact has, different roles and self-relations: a legal person, a moral subject, a member of a family and corporation, a citizen in the state. The common ground of different rights makes it possible to conceive the system of rights as a genuine system. It also makes it possible to conceive the relations and transitions between the forms of will in such a way that the transition to a higher form is not abrupt, but follows logically from the preceding stages.

For Hegel, it is essential that the modern state entails spheres for particular interests, for moral choice and reflection, and for the recognition of subjective capacities. These could be defined as the negative rights of the liberal tradition. On the other hand, these rights do not remain abstract demands but are continuously realized. This cannot happen without collisions and without the subordination of rights to each other. However, this subordination, and ultimately the substantial unity of *Rechtsgemeinschaft*, is entailed in the principle of subjectivity. Without free subjectivity, we cannot conceive of right

(*Recht*); without right there would be no unity of ethical life – unity in the sense that ethical powers are not something alien, and rights not something formed outside the realization of our freedom.

Notes

[1] All citations of Hegels text are from *Elements of the Philosophy of Right*. Ed. Allen Wood, transl. H.B.Nisbet. Cambridge University Press 1991.

[2] Hegel uses the term 'person' here in a sense analogous to his discussion on abstract right, the principle of which is: "be a person and respect others as persons" (*PR* § 36). The term person presupposes a starting point which is abstracted from all concrete and substantial relations between subjects. This is true in the case of the family as a person, too. However, this independence is only a starting point and possibility for concrete economic and other relations. See *PR* §§ 162, 170–172.

[3] A careful discussion of Hegel's conception of the family can be found in Michael O. Hardimon 1994. *Hegel's social philosophy. The project of reconciliation*. Cambridge University Press (esp. pp. 175–189).

[4] Determined particularity as an expression and realization of one's freedom (of moral subjectivity) is explicated in Siep, L. 1992. 'Was heisst: "Aufhebung der Moralität in Sittlichkeit" in Hegels Rechtsphilosophie', *Praktische Philosophie im Deutschen Idealismus*, Suhrkamp, Frankfurt/M (esp. pp. 231–3); Wood, A. 1991. *Hegel's Ethical Thought*. Cambridge University Press (esp. pp. 239–241).

[5] *PR* § 183, §§ 189–195. On the conceptualization of the system of needs as a locus of 'aufgehoben' subjective morality, see Siep 1992, 231. The empty demand of moral subjectivity for the welfare of all gains reality in the mutual dependence of needs – although quite unintentionally.

[6] Steven B. Smith 1989. *Hegel's Critique of Liberalism*. p.143.

[7] It should be noted, however, that this aspect of positively conceived freedom does not require the 'materialization of law'. The rights and duties of corporations and their members function within the sphere of civil society. Thus, for example, it is not a subject's duty to support the state economically, any more than it is the state's duty to support individuals economically. In this sense it is important to differentiate between the modern welfare state with its conception of rights and this ethical dimension inside the Hegelian civil society.

[8] The form in which Hegel expresses this in his lectures on the philosophy of history does not suggest a descriptive illumination of history, but a systematic explanation of the principle underlying it. In the New World the form of freedom is one which "has its own absolute itself as its purport". *The Philosophy of History*, transl. by J. Sibree. Prometheus books 1991. p. 341.

[9] This kind of view is held, for example, by Jürgen Habermas in his book *The Philosophical Discourse of Modernity*. Cambridge MA, M.I.T. Press 1987. esp. pp. 36,42. Hegel's solution "overpowers every [finite] absolutization and retains as unconditional only the infinite prosessing of the relation-to-self that swallows up everything finite within itself" (p. 42). A well-grounded criticism to this view is presented by Robert B. Pippin: "Hegel, Modernity, and Habermas". *The Monist* 74/2 1991, pp. 329–357.

[10] See Pippin, p. 339 ff. Here I cannot follow Pippin's argument of Hegel's theoretical self-grounding of modernity in detail,but I try to show how this principle is at work in in *PR*, a work which is most often seen as a sign of an accommodational stagnation of Hegel's thought.

[11] Hegel, *Enzyklopädie der philosophischen Wissenschaften I*, §§ 213–215.

[12] The origin of Hegel's concept of right and its relation to the alternatives of the political thought of early modernity is carefully discussed in: Manfred Riedel: 'Laws of Nature and Laws of Right: Problems in the Realization of Freedom', *Between Tradition and Revolution*, Cambridge University Press 1984, pp. 57–75.

[13] According to Hegel, this limiting oneself to sheer objectivity belongs to certain historical periods and forms of will: "...we may also describe as objective the will which is completely immersed in its object, such as the will of the child, which is founded on trust and lacks subjective freedom, and the will of the slave, which does not yet know itself as free and is consequently a will with no will of its own. In this sense, every will whose actions are guided by an alien authority and which has not yet completed its infinite return into itself is objective." (*PR* § 26 *Addition* [*Zusatz*])

[14] "In a fully organized state, it is only a question of the highest instance of the formal decision, and all that is required in a monarch is someone to say 'yes' and dot the 'i';..." (*PR* § 280, *Addition*)

Eerik Lagerspetz

HEGEL AND HOBBES ON THE SOVEREIGNTY OF THE PEOPLE

In most issues related to political philosophy, Thomas Hobbes and Georg Wilhelm Friedrich Hegel seem to represent the opposite poles. There is no reason to enumerate their disagreements; instead, I would like to point out one issue on which they agreed. Both were opponents of the Sovereignty of the People in all its forms. Both rejected all attempts to construct a right to resistance, a right of the people to disobey their rulers, to depose them, or to change the existing mode of government. Moreover, the structure of the arguments they employed in this context were similar. The core of their arguments was, I think, this: *the People had no independent existence outside the positive institutions. Hence, it could not possess any rights which were independent of those institutions.* This amounted a rejection of the whole "democratic" orientation of the modern theories of Natural Law.

In one sense, it is not quite correct to ascribe the idea of popular sovereignty to authors who wrote before Locke and Rousseau. Nevertheless, the Neo-Scholastic theorists like Suarez, the Protestant Monarcomachs like Althusius and Buchanan and the British parliamentary publicists before and during the Civil War shared the idea that "the People" existed before the creation of the State, and that it was in a reciprocial, contract-like relationship between its rulers. Hence, it was conceptually meaningful to ask what rights the people possessed *vis-à-vis* its rulers. Which were the terms of the original contract? Had the people a right to judge the actions of the prince? Might the people disobey him, actively resist him, an in the case of extreme tyranny, even depose and punish him in a lawful way? And the most radical question was, of course: if the People was the origin of the power, could it change the existing mode of government at will? The early contract theorists disagreed over these issues, but the questions themselves were conceived as meaningful.

During and after the French Revolution these questions were again presented in a new and more radical form. The basic difference between the early 17th and the late 18th century discourses was the new notion of the Constitution as a basic law which was, unlike the old Fundamental Laws, written, above the ordinary legislation, and amendable only in a specified way. Another new element was the the notion of the *pouvoir constituant* as the fundamental and final authority which stood behind all positive institutions.

Hobbes' Argument

The common understanding in the 17th century was that all political obligations were established in a reciprocal contract between the rulers and their subjects. The defenders of absolutism – Suarez, Grotius and Bodin – tried to argue that the nature of this contract was an unconditional *translatio* rather than a conditional *concessio*, so that the people did not reserve the ultimate power to themselves (Suarez 1612/1944, III.iv.6.; Grotius 1625/1853, I.iii.viii). But there were obvious problems in this argument. Firstly, in the absence of any factual evidence, wasn't it more natural to suppose that the people was ultimately the more powerful contract partner? After all, there could be peoples without kings but no kings without the people. Secondly, human beings generally enter into contractual relationships for the sake of some benefit. This would imply that the people as a contract partner would have right to renounce the contract at least in the extreme cases, in the cases of immediate necessity – and, wanting a supreme judge, only the people itself could judge the nature of the situation. The most the contract-oriented absolutists could show was that an unconditional *translatio* was *one possible* mode of the Original Contract, as Sir Robert Filmer remarked (Filmer 1652/1991, 223-224). The status of the ruler became a contingent matter: it was dependent on the terms of the original contract.

In his defence of absolutism, Hobbes accepted the contract postulate, but gave it a completely new meaning. In a nutshell, his argument is the following: The only actors in the world are (i) natural individuals and (ii) artificial persons. An artificial person exists only when the natural individuals which constitute it have authorized representatives which have a right to act on behalf of them. An artificial person can act only when its representatives act (Hobbes 1651/1973, ch. xiv).

Now, "the people" cannot refer but to an artificial person. Hence, the people can act only through it representatives. Hence, we cannot meaningfully say that the people could act *against* its representatives. The (sole) representative of the people is the Sovereign, established in the original contract. And because of this it is not meaningful to say that the people, as a collective, can have a right to act against their Sovereign. This becomes clear in the case of a democracy, in which whole the people, organized as a sovereign decision making body, acts as its own representative. In this limiting case, it is clearly meaningless to say that the people has rights against itself. But the situation is not different in other modes of government. In a monarchy, the people can be said to have rights against the king only if the people can exercize them as an organized collective, e.g. as a democratic assembly. But then, *this assembly is the true representative, against which there cannot be any further rights*, and the true mode of government is not monarchical, but a democratic one. (Hobbes 1651/1973, 95)

If you take away the representives, natural individuals do not constitute an artificial person; they are only as many individuals. Thus they can act,express their will, and be possessors of rights only as individuals. An unorganized multitude does not do anything and has no normative status *as a group*. If the supreme representatives, those of a Commonwealth, are taken away, its citizens return to the State of Nature. According to Hobbes' paradoxical expression "the People does not make the King; the King makes the People". Hobbes presents an ontological and action-theoretical argument which has important political consequences.

What Hegel Means by 'Constitution'?

Substantial parts of Hegel's *Elements of the Philosophy of Right* (*PR*) are directed against various doctrines of popular sovereignty. The arguments are essentially interconnected with Hegel's theory of monarchy, and the latter, which has puzzled some commentators, becomes much more clear if we read it in this context. Hegel was as frightened by the spectre of revolution as Hobbes. They made the same diagnosis: the ultimate consequence of a popular revolution would not be the emergence of a new order, but a pulverized society, chaos and confusion, a state of nature (*Enc.*, § 502). It is significant that the latter term does appear in Hegel's text, and it is used in its specifically Hobbesian meaning, as a *post-social state* characterized by conflict and disorder.

Hegel's term for constitution was *Verfassung*, which did not have the revolutionary connotations of the alternative term *Konstitution*. Both terms, however, were ambiguous in the same way. In the beginning of the 19th century, *Verfassung* could still refer either to a written document, or to the totality of those rules and practices which constituted the basic structure of the State. (Jyränki 1989, 197-8) It is clear that Hegel used the term in its latter, more traditional meaning. But he used it with a special emphasis. For him, a constitution was not only "the organization of the state", but also "the process of its [the State's] organic life with reference to itself" (*PR* § 271). Thus, a constitution was not simply a set of rules and practices.

This *processual* definition of constitution is plausible for several reasons. Suppose, for the argument's sake, that we define the constitution – say, of Finland – as the set of those norms and practices which organize the basic structure of the State *at a given moment*. The problem with this definition is that it is by no means clear whether we can actually identify the elements of the set. At any given moment, some constitutional practices can be open, uncertain and contested. Thus, for some possible elements, we cannot really say whether they belong to the set or not. Was, for example, the practice of constitutional review a part of the US constitution from the start? Or was is established only in 1820 by the famous decision in the *Marbury vs. Madison* case? Or was it established even later, when it become common and usual practice?

Moreover, consider the problem of identification of a constitution in different times. If constitutions are defined as sets of norms, Finland had different constitutions in 1936, 1976 and 1996. Nevertheless, we think that there exists an entity called "the Finnish constitution", which has preserved its identity in spite of the changes. Derogations, amendments, and changes in constitutional practices do not mean that the constitution has changed its identity. Should we say that the constitution should be defined as a set of the successive sets of constitutional norms? What should those sets to have in common in order to form a continuous whole? What makes them elements of the *same* constitution? It is not just a matter of similarity: a pre- and a post-revolutionary constitution, for example, may have many common elements.

Should we say that two successive sets of norms belong to the same constitution if the norms of the earlier set justify or authorize the norms of the later set, as is the case of a constitution amended in the normal order? Is legal *continuity* the decisive criterion for the identification of a constitution? The problem with this proposal is that such a relation may prevail even between entities which certainly should be conceived as separate constitutions. For example, the constitutions of the British Dominions derive their justification from the British constitution, but they are not parts of it.

One may try to save the definition based on continuity by saying that two successive sets of norms belong to the same constitution if the temporally earlier set authorizes the later one *and* they are spatially coextensive (i.e. claim authority over the same geographical area). But consider the case of Bulgaria or Hungary before and after the recent political changes. The legal continuity was preserved; new constitutions were accepted by using the procedures of the old Socialist constitutions. However, the countries have gone through radical political changes. It is implausible to say that they have the same constitutions they had before the recent changes.

Thus, we should be able to identify a constitution so that (1) *any* part of it can be changed while it preserves its identity, (2) *all* important parts of it may, in the course of time, change while it still preserves its identity, but (3) *some* changes may cause a loss of identity. Any attempt to identify a constitution as a set of norms, or as a set of such sets, produces a sort of "Zeno's paradox" in legal theory: gradual change which nevertheless preserves the identity of the changing object is inexplicable. Hegel's way to characterize constitutions as *processes* is a natural alternative[1]. Constitutions do develop, they are not created by a single act:

> For a constitution is not simply made; it is the work of centuries, the Idea and consciousness of the rational (in so far as the consciousness is developed in a nation). No constitution can therefore be created purely subjectively [von Subjekten]. (*PR*, Addition to § 274)

The last sentence is especially significant. No single will can create the "organism" which makes the common will possible. (cf. *Enc.* § 540). This holds true with the rulers as well as with the People. An *octroyed* constitution which is based only on the unilateral will of the prince is as impossible as a constitution created by an unilateral act of the People.

The Argument against the Sovereignty of the People

In *Philosophie des Rechts*, the apparent aim of Hegel's arguments against the doctrine of popular sovereignty is Rousseau (and Fichte). His reading of Rousseau is characteristically one-sided, and, following the common notion of his time, he makes Rousseau's philosophy responsible for the Terror (*PR* § 258). The real target standing behind Rousseau is, then, the spirit of 1789: the proponents of the Revolution asserted that the People or *la nation* had an inalienable and permanent right to dissolve the political bond between its rulers and write a new Constitution, conceived as a blueprint of the whole society. In his *Qu'est-ce que le Tiers État?* Emmanuel Sieyès declares:

> Non seulement la nation n'est pas soumise à une constitution, mais elle ne *peut* pas l'être, mais elle ne *doit* pas l'être, ce qui équivaut encore à dire qu'elle ne l'est pas. (...) On doit concevoir les nations sur la terre comme des individus hors du lien social, ou comme l'on dit, dans l'ètat de nature. L'exercice de leur volonté est libre et indépendent de toutes formes civiles. N'existant que dans l'ordre naturel, leur volonté, pour sortir tout son effet, n'a besoin que de porter les caractères *naturels* d'une volonté. De quelque manière qu'un nation veuille, il suffit qu'elle veuille; toutes formes sont bonnes, et sa volonté est toujours la loi supréme. (pp. 68-9)

For Sieyès, *la nation* is at same time independent of all positive laws and their only source. When exercizing its original constitutive power, the nation or the people cannot, for conceptual reasons, be bound by any positive law or existing tradition. Here we have Hegel's answer:

> Another question readily presents itself here: 'Who is to draw up the constitution?' This question seems clear enough, but closer inspection at once shows that it is nonsensical. For it presup-

poses that no constitution as yet exists, so that only an atomistic aggregate of individuals is present. How such a aggregate could arrive at a constitution, whether by its own devices or with out- side help, through altruism [Güte], thought, or force, would have to be left to it to decide, for the concept is not applicable to an aggregate. But if the above question presupposes a constitution is already present, to draw up a constitution can only mean to change it, and the very fact that a constitution is presupposed at once implies that this change could take place only in a constitu- tional manner. (*PR* § 273; cf. *Enc.* § 540)

Every group of individuals either has a constitution (in the wide sense defined above) or does not have it. If it has one, the constitution provides, at least in princple, means to amend itself. This does not presuppose the existence and use of an explicit amendment rule; momentous constitutional changes are often made through a gradual change of practices (consider the breakthrough of parliamentarism in the most West European monarchies). But if some group has no constitution, it is only an agglomeration of individuals who cannot articulate any common will. They may perhaps create themselves a constitution, but there cannot be any established way to do it, other- wise they would already have a constitution. In neither case, there is no point to appeal to the People as the *pouvoir constituant*, as a necessary authority behind the constitution.

Consider an example. The members of *le Tiers État* declared themselves as the Constitutional Convention which was free to cre- ate a new constitution for France, disregarding all existing laws and traditions. But how did they acquire their authority as the repre- sentatives of the Nation? By which manner were they going to make decisions? They were elected as representatives according to some rules (actually, according to those of the ancient constitution), and they were forced to use some decision procedure (e.g. majority rule) in their decision making. The same would hold true in respect with any conceivable constitutional convention; even if whole the French Nation were to met and to choose itself a constitution, it would equally need some pre-existing rules of decision making. These rules could be taken as binding only because they were in some way rooted in the existing practices. In a sense the French nation could give itself a constitution only if it already possessed a constitution. And, the history of the French Revolution seems to show that the French nation was actually unable to accomplish the task – for the very reason, Hegel might say, that it tried to break itself out from the existing constitutional tradition. The force of Hegel's argument is in the observation that no social arrangement can be created *ex nihilo*, in a social vacuum. There could be no empty space, no state of nature, between old and new constitutions[2]. Nevertheless, because political institutions were not originally established by God, the only remaining alternative seemed to be that they have been developed gradually and unintentionally, but in a rational way. Thus, adherence to a constitutional tradition does not involve a blind submission to it. It consists of recognizing its reasonable elements, of developing a tradition rather than accepting or rejecting it unconditionally. This view, I think, is characterististical of Hegel's whole philosophy: we cannot just step outside our received beliefs and practices, nor can we give up our ability to reflect them critically.

We see how the processual definition of constitution was linked to the denial of popular sovereignty. Because a constitution is not simply an artifice fully established at a given moment, it cannot be considered as a product of a single will. The constitution of the State defines the role and the power of the State organs. It cannot, for the reasons presented above, give any rights to the People without specifying how, when, and according to which procedure the People were to exercize those rights. Hence, "the People", without any concrete determination, cannot not have any political role at all. The People, like the ruler, was a creation of positive institutions. Here, the similarity with Hobbes' argument is clear.

Hegel's Argument for Monarchy

More problematically, Hegel also thought that the necessity of a *monarchical* constitution could be derived from similar considerations.

But the usual sense in which the term 'popular sovereignty' has begun to be used in recent times is to denote the opposite of that sovereignty which exists in the monarch. In this oppositional sense, popular sovereignty is one of those confused thoughts which are based on a garbled notion [*Vorstellung*] of the people. Without its monarch and that articulation of the whole which is necessarily and immediately associated with monarchy, the people is a formless mass. The latter is no longer a state an none of those determinations which are encountered only in an internally organized whole (such as sovereignty, government, courts of law, public authorities [*Obrigkeit*], estates, etc.) is applicable to it. It is only when moments such as these which refer to an organization, to political life, emerge in a people that it ceases to be an indeterminate abstraction which the purely general idea [Vorstellung] of the people denotes. (*PR* § 279)

The last part of the quoted passage repeats the argument on the necessity of a constitution (in the wide sense discussed above). The first part contains the basic argument I ascribed to Hobbes: the fact that individuals are united by a common ruler makes them a people, not the other way round. Hence it is impossible to say that they have a right against their ruler. Certainly, the arguments fit together. Common rules and traditions are not as such sufficient to create a state. There must be an ultimate way to make decisions, an authoritative instance which guarantees that rules and traditions are mutually consistent. An argument based on the need of the final decision maker was, of course, essential to Hobbes, and after him, for the whole theory of sovereignty as it developed in jurisprudence and in political theory. In a cryptical-sounding remark to *PR* § 280, Hegel relates his proof of the necessity of monarchy to the ontological proof of the existence of God (Hegel, as we remember, was not satisfied with Kant's refutation of the proof). Now, I have tried to show elsewhere how the classical theory of Sovereignty, from Hobbes onward, relied on an argument which was structurally similar to the ontological argument in theology. Because all norms and decisions inside a political community were expressions of will backed by power, there ought, for purely conceptual reasons, to be a supreme and final will in any Commonwealth (Lagerspetz 1995, ch. 6.). It is possible that Hegel had something similar in his mind. If the law was an expression of will, there ought to be the final, ultimate will in the constitution of a State governed by law. The difference between a Hobbesian and a Hegelian monarch was that although a Hegelian monarch had the right of *ultimate* discretion, he did not have *unlimited* discretion.

In Hegel's philosophy of law, the sovereignty[3] is ascribed, not to the ruler, but to a collective being, the State. This was a conceptual innovation, and only much later it became a commonplace in the German legal theory (Jyränki 1989, 209-210; 231-232). For Hegel, the State is capable to possess a will and to act. But like a Hobbesian artificial person, it cannot will and act unless some natural individuals also will and act. Ultimately, the State as an artifical person has a will only if there exists a single will of a natural individual which clearly and unambiguously represents the will of the State. (cf. *Int.*, 116) That individual will is not supposed to be arbitrary or capricious: in the ideal case, it has no role but to draw the inescapable conclusion following from rational arguments, and to declare it in public. This does not make the individual will merely a rubber stamp. Hegel's monarch has no active role, not because his power is restricted by constitutional norms but, because, in the ideal State with its ideal administration, he *need* not to do much.

Peter J. Steinberger (1988) has provided an interpretation of Hegel which is akin to my own. We regularily say that collectivities – the University, for example – perform actions. We also think that they can be held responsible of something they have done. But they cannot perform what Arthur C. Danto (1968) calls *basic actions*, say, bodily movements. Actions of other types must ultimately presuppose some basic actions which constitute the more complex ones.

Now, one may claim that Danto's (and Steinberger's) notion of actions which are basic in some absolute sense is metaphysically dubious, and potentially incompatible with Hegel's theory of action[4]. Fortunately, we have no need to go deeper into that issue. In order to present the argument, we need only to recognize that some actions are more basic *in respect with some other actions*. For example, making a decision in a collectivity is necessarily constituted by some other actions, e.g. individual voting acts. Voting, in its turn, is constituted by e.g. raising hands, saying "Aye" or "Nay", or writing on a slip. No absolute notion of basicness of actions is needed.

The actions ascribed to collectives are necessarily constituted by more basic actions perfomed by their members. But not any action will do. Only actions of some members of the University, performed in some contexts, are counted as actions of the University or of its administrative sub-units. If I vote in the Council of my Faculty, my act, toghether with the similar acts perfomed by the other members of the Council, constitutes a part of the actions performed by the Faculty. But if I steal some property of the University, the Faculty has not stealed anything. This is because there are rules and conventions – the "constitution" of the Faculty – specifying which individual actions, performed in which type of contexts, are counted as actions of the Faculty. The same holds with the State and its agents. Steinberger explains:

> For Hegel, political society must be conceived of as an autonomous, rational agent, an entity capable of acting in the fullest sense; for otherwise it would merely operate out of some kind of natural principle, thereby failing to fulfill the requirements of freedom, both for itself and for its members. But further, such a society cannot be conceived of merely as a collectivity, for collectives cannot perform basic actions and cannot plausibly be held responsible for actions they perform. If then, political society is to be an actor, it must be conceived in terms of a single, real human being; and this human being is the monarch. Louis XIV's claim that "L'état c'est moi", is, I believe, adopted by Hegel as an analytically true principle of political society. In a very real sense, the state *is* the monarch; hence, the state is an actor – autonomous and responsible – only insofar as the monarch is too. (Steinberger 1988, 220)

This is actually the Hobbesian theory of the actions of artificial persons. But there is a problem in Hegel's version of it. Hobbes never said that his preference for monarchy would follow from the argument – indeed, in the Preface in *De Cive* he explicitly says that it does *not* follow from it. A Hobbesian "representative" of a political society can be a monarch, an aristocratic chamber, or even an assembly of all the citizens. The conceptual argument shows that "representatives" are necessary, but it does not pick any particular structure of representation. Hegel's theory, as well as Hobbes', implies that the sovereignty or the ultimate power cannot belong to an unorganized collection of individuals. But why could not an elected ruler, a representative assembly, or a general meeting of all citizens, perform the task of willing and acting? In the form presented by Steinberger, the argument would imply that not only the State but *every* human organization ought to have "monarchical" structure in order to will, act, or to be held responsible for something. Why political society should "be conceived in terms of *a single, real human being*" if other organizations can be conceived in terms of several human beings – in terms of councils, boards, collegia etc.?

Conclusion

Much ink has been spilled on the question whether Hegel should be considered as a conservative, liberal, or radical thinker. The question, I think, is meaningful only when considered in some particular context, and the most relevant context here is his position in the constitutional debate of the early19th century. The Congress of Vienna (1814-5) created the German League, and made detailed decisions concerning the contents of the constitutions of its member states[5]. All German States were ordered to have a monarchical constitution and a representative assembly in which the landed nobility had a predominant role. Some concessions, however, had to be made to the liberal bourgoisie. These requirements were laid down by Metternicht's secretary, Friedrich von Gentz. Gentz, like his master, was a pragmatic conservative; his orientation was a Burkean one (he actually translated Burke's *Reflections*). The great aim of

Metternicht and von Gentz was to preserve the European balance of power and the internal order of the States; their model for the German constitutions was the French *Charte* of 1814 – a document which rejected the idea of popular sovereignty, but which still did not satisfy the most extreme legitimists. (See Jyränki 1989, chs. vi-viii)

In this context, Hegel was clearly a moderate liberal (or, if we like, a liberal conservative). Unlike the extreme legitimists (say, de Maistre or von Haller), Hegel was a constitutionalist; unlike the more moderate legitimists (like von Gentz), he did not believe that a constitution could be *octroyed*, be given by the unilateral act of the Ruler; unlike the radicals, he did not accept the idea that it could be created by the people *ex nihilo*. He rejected the two traditional solutions to the sovereignty problem. Sovereignty did not belong either to the ruler or to the people: it belonged to the State from which both derived their existence. (In *Introduction to the Philosophy of History*, this solution was presented as a characteristic Hegelian *Aufhebung* of opposites.) Hegel was painfully aware that the traditional solutions could be and actually were used as justifications for arbitrary despotism. The question is whether his own solution, making the State as the locus of sovereignty, contained the seeds of even more frightening forms of despotism. In the legal theory of the emerging German *Reich*, the role of the notion of the State sovereignty became essential. Using the infinite wisdom of hindsight, we may see Hegel's role as the father (or rather, as the midwife) of the notion of state sovereignty as a link – perhaps as the only link – between his political philosophy and the modern authoritarian State[6].

Has the argument presented by Hegel and Hobbes any contemporary relevancy? Consider the question of the right to national self-determination, the modern version of popular sovereignty recognized e.g. by the fundamental charter of the United Nations. Which groups are the possessors of this fundamental right – the Yugoslavs, the Bosnians, the Bosnian Serbs, the Bosnian Muslims living amongst the Bosnian Serbs? When we are entitled to say that a non-independent nation wants to exercise that right? How do we recognize the "authentic" expression of the will of a people, if the democratic institutions do not already exist? To quote Juha Räikkä (1996, 59) "one cannot reasonably ask from the people whether they constitute a people. If one to knows to whom the question should be addressed, one also knows who constitute the people, and there is no need to ask the question at all". The people can meaningfully exercise a right only in some pre-existing institutional context. Hegel and Hobbes would certainly recognize this line of argument as their own. And, in the theory of democracy, it still points out a real problem.

Notes

[1] I do not deny that we may use the term "constitution" in a more limited sense. Nevertheless, our normal usage – when, for example, we refer to "the US Constitution" – seems to be quite near to Hegel's use of the term. – On closely related problem of the legal continuity, see John Finnis (1973).

[2] Hegel's comments could be compared with the penetrating analysis of the constitutional ideologies of the American and the French Revolutions made by Hannah Arendt in her *On Revolution*, see espec. ch. 4.

[3] The German language had no term for sovereignty before the Napoleonic era. The Rhine Confederation in 1806 is one of the first legal documents which uses the term *Souveranetät* (Hinsley 1986, 137). – On Hegel's notion of sovereignty, see Petersen 1992, 147-169.

[4] I owe this point to Dr. Michael Quante.

[5] The content of these decision was specified in the Viennese *Schlussakte* in 1820. Hegel's Prussia did not, of course, have a written constitution at all before 1850.

[6] An example of this is Giovanni Gentile's theory, inspired by Hegel, that the society is a creation of the State (Gentile 1946/1963).

Sources

Enc.   *Encylopaedia of the Philosophical Sciences. Vol. 3. Philosophy of Mind.* Transl. W. Wallace, Clarendon Press, Oxford 1971.

Int.   *Lectures on the Philosophy of World History. Introduction: Reason in World History.* Transl. H.B. Nisbet. Cambridge University Press, Cambridge 1980.

PR   Elements of the Philosophy of Right. Transl. H. B. Nisbet. Cambridge University Press, Cambridge 1991.
Hegel's Werke 1.-20. Suhrkamp, Frankfurt am Main 1986.

Literature

Arendt, Hannah (1963/1982) *On Revolution.* Penguine Books, Harmodsworth.

Danto, Arthur C. (1968) 'Basic Actions'in A. R. White (ed.), *The Philosophy of Action.* Oxford University Press, Oxford.

Filmer, Sir Robert (1653/1991) 'Observations Concerning the Original of Government' in *Patriarcha and Other Writings.* Ed. J. P. Sommerville, Cambridge University Press, Cambridge.

Finnis, John (1973) 'Revolutions and Continuity of Law' in A.W.B. Simpson (ed.) *Oxford Essays on Jurisprudence 2.*, Oxford University Press, Oxford, 50-61.

Gentile, Giovanni (1946/1963) *Genesis and Structure of Society.* Tr. H. Harris. Illinois University Press, Urbana.

Grotius, Hugo (1625/1853) *The Rights of Peace and War.* Ed. W. Whewell. Cambridge University Press, Cambridge.

Hinsley, F.H. (1986) *Sovereignty.* Cambridge University Press, Cambridge.

Hobbes, Thomas (1658/1972) *Man and Citizen.* Humanities Press, New York.

Hobbes, Thomas (1651/1973) *Leviathan.* Dent, London.

Jyränki, Antero (1989) *Lakien laki.* Lakimiesliiton kustannus, Helsinki.

Lagerspetz, Eerik (1995) *The Opposite Mirrors.* Dordrecht, Kluwer.

Petersen, Thomas (1992) *Subjektivität und Politik.* Athenäums Monographien, Frankfurt am Main.

Räikkä, Juha (1996) 'Hyvä ja paha kansainvälisessä politiikassa', in E. Lagerspetz, H. Patomäki and J. Räikkä, *Maailmanpolitiikan moraali.* Edita, Helsinki.

Sieyès, Emmanuel (1789/1982) *Qu'est-ce que le Tiers État?* Quadrige/PUF, Paris.

Steinberger, Peter J. (1988) *Logic and Politics. Hegel's Philosophy of Right.* Yale University Press, New Haven.

Suarez, Francisco (1612/1944) *De legibus ac Deo legislatore*, in Williams et al. (eds.) *Selections from Three Works of Francisco Suarez*, Clarendon Press, Oxford.

Hannu Sivenius

REMARKS ON SCHELLING'S CRITICISM OF THE HEGELIAN IDEA OF THE STATE

I t has often been said that Schelling's later philosophy (the so-called "Spätphilosophie") represents a continual criticism of Hegelian philosophy (e.g. Fuhrmans 1956a, 296). In his article "Das Verhältnis des späten Schelling zu Hegel", Walter Schulz already emphasized that "the peculiar nature of Schelling's later philosophy can only be grasped if one takes the philosophy of Hegel as a starting point for critique and if one accepts that Schelling's later philosophy is a fundamental critique of Hegel's own philosophy" (Schulz 1954, 343; for a more extensive historical and systematic analysis of this issue, see Habermas 1954, 16-119). Schelling seems to have been deeply convinced that the philosophy of Hegel was merely "logical", and that it was antithetical to a philosophy which was "historical" in the true sense of the word. Perhaps it can be said that for Hegel philosophy is based on a kind of *Aufhebungsdialektik*, whereas for Schelling it represents an *Erzeugungsdialektik*, as Edward Allen Beach has recently suggested in his study of Schelling's philosophy of mythology (Beach 1994, 83-91; cf. Schelling 1856/61, XI, 330; VIII, 289- and XI, 488, 522, 562). During his stay in Munich (from 1827 onwards), the concept of "true philosophy" was most important for Schelling, whereas after moving to Berlin he began to regard philosophy as a kind of duality in unity (*Zweiheit in der Einheit*), as a kind of synthesis between historical and logical, or positive and negative philosophy.

Schelling criticized Hegel very sharply in his late philosophy, incorporating Hegel's philosophy of the state in his criticism. It is striking that the lectures given by Schelling on the history of modern philosophy do not include this critique of the Hegelian concept of the state. However, in 1833/34 Schelling gave a series of lectures on the "Geschichte der philosophischen Systeme von Cartesius bis auf die gegenwärtige Zeit als Übergang zum System der positiven Philosophie", a transcript of which is in the possession of Horst Fuhrmans and which has been partly published by Alexander Hollerbach (in his *Der Rechtsgedanke bei Schelling*). From these lectures it can be seen that Schelling not only criticized Hegel's conception of the state, but also developed his own thesis concerning the state – one which was to be a recurrent theme in his letters to Maximilian. (See Fuhrmans 1956b, 304, and Fuhrmans 1955, 286 and 386). In this context of criticism against Hegel's logical mode of doing philosophy, the formulation of Frauenstädt is very typical: "Hegel gives us invalid paper money and creates the impression that it is a treasure, but a single historical fact is worth more than his whole logic, because we have to refer to *history* first of all" (Frauenstädt 1842, 131).

I

In the above-mentioned series of lectures Schelling first attacks Hegel's conception of religion and art. He makes it quite clear that religion and art ought to be understood as autonomous spheres and not as representing purely intermediary phases. In particular Schelling objected to the typically rationalistic assumption that the essence of religion consists in a doctrine, be it moral or theoretical. Schelling was at pains to demonstrate that the religion of our prehistoric ancestors was not of a doctrinal nature at all, whereas that of more developed cultures always consists of an inseparable synthesis between doctrine and actuality. Schelling never accepted the Hegelian interpretation of religion as representation. According to him, the myths that a religion contained were nothing but pictorial representations (Vorstellungen) of a content that only philosophical reason can adequately grasp. Gradually he came to distance himself increasingly from all interpretations of religion as standing for something else, something that in itself would supposedly be without a divine nature.

Schelling then goes on to state: "(In Hegel) everything that has been considered valuable from the beginning of humanity is treated with contempt. In contrast to this, his philosophy ends with an absolute divinization of the state". When history, art and poetry have all disappeared, the state remains. It is still there, as flourishing as ever before. According to Schelling, when speculative thought is fully reborn, it has only the state against it. The reason for this is that the state is in itself the purest expression of speculative thought. Schelling says that it is quite correct to accuse Hegelian philosophy of servility or servitude (*Servilismus*). For him it is easy to see that the Hegelian concept of state contains every characteristic of illiberalism (*Illiberalismus*). In its divinization of the state, Hegelian philosophy gets tangled with the typical errors to which such a divinization leads even today. Moreover, monarchists and antimonarchists largely presuppose this differentiation and elevation of the state. The state, Schelling emphasizes, belongs to the "negative side" (like religion, art and science), even though it contains many positive things. Furthermore, the state is only a *conditio sine qua non* of a better and higher life. In our attempt to reach true freedom, we ought to limit the state in relation to this better and higher life. Schelling emphasizes that we must always remember that the state has only servile functions. We should not make the state an end (*Zweck*), because the state is never an end in itself.

Schelling claims that if a human being is sane, he does not feel his organic side or his own organism. If someone thinks that his own organism is an end (*Zweck*) to himself, then he must already be sick. Analogously, Schelling says, a people which has to strive for the preservation of its own organism is also sick and has sunk onto a lower level of development. Generally speaking, at this lower level discontentedness (*Missbehagen*) reigns. From this it follows that the true task of our time is to limit the functioning of the state. The scope of the state must be limited, not only in its monarchical form but in its entirety.

If I am a poisoner (*Giftbecher*), it is all the same to me whether I am convicted in a state with a monarchical constitution or in a state with a constitution based on philosophical or democratic principles. Furthermore, if the task is to limit the state itself, then e.g. in a monarchical state the situation cannot be such that the monarch is limited by the people or the people by the monarch. If this were the case, it would only create duality and confusion. Schelling holds on to the view that if the state is limited in itself, then the monarch or the people – understood as political elements – are also limited. Why? A possible answer to this question might be found in the idea that the monarch has unlimited power in his own sphere of functioning. Schelling seems to draw the conclusion that if the monarch does not have power in certain areas of society, it is because the state does not have that power. Consequently, the power which the monarch has, or which he can exercise, can only be the right of the state itself. So if a person (i.e. Hegel) wants to make the state the highest possible power, then that person blows the state out of every reasonable proportion, and his philosophical system is essentially illiberal in the true sense of the word. This conclusion is necessary, because illiberalism means that everything that truly belongs to the realm of freedom is suppressed by the state. This, at least, is Schelling's view. He further claims that Hegel's famous statement "Whatever is rational is actual and vice versa..." (*PR*, 10) is a clear expression of this illiberalism. To this famous dictum of Hegel, Schelling retorted sharply: "If reason is *all* of being (and hence, conversely, all being is reason), then there is no difficulty in introducing unreason, which yet is necessary in order to explain the actual world" (Schelling 1856/61, XIV, 23).

Shelling's fundamental thesis in his lecture series mentioned above is that the state is the *conditio sine qua non* of higher life. He later repeats this thesis in his purely rational (*reinrationale*) system of philosophy and in his letters to Maximilian. The state belongs to the realm of negative philosophy. Its task is to be the vehicle of the positive, higher form of life. The state ought to make this higher form of life possible, but, considered in itself, the state is only a formal structure within the system of negative philosophy. The state is not an end in itself. Not any more. According to Schelling, this is the way in which the state must be understood. This is the only way in which true freedom can be preserved, the freedom which is necessarily involved in the development of the spirit. By contrast, the divinization of the state leads to a misunderstanding of true freedom. In other words, it leads to illiberalism.

This seems to lead us back to the classical liberalistic and individualistic thesis of the "night-watchman state" (Nachtwächterstaat). For example, Wilhelm von Humboldt was of the opinion that Schelling's theory is an attempt to define the limits of the functions of the state. It must be borne in mind, however, that Schelling does not want to fall back to the trap of an individualistic theory nor to the view developed in his earlier article "Neue Deduktion des Naturrechts" (1796). Schelling later defined the community based on law as a community of different estates – this time, however, developing the idea of the state as an organism. The state is, in fact, conceived of as something more than an "external organism", because without it true spiritual life would be impossible.

The role of the state is foundational. Yet the state must not be considered as an essence, for it has only servile functions. Here Schelling uses certain naturalistic analogies. He says that the functioning of the state can be compared with that of the body with its different organs. All the organs and members of the body are essential, because together they make possible the development of the spirit. The free individuality of the spirit can only develop itself on the basis of the communal state which limits it. In the same way, the free individuality of the spirit must rise above the organism which limits it. Thus, Schelling is not satisfied with an individualistic conception of the state. He is equally unsatisfied with the liberalistic theory of it, in which the state is understood as a "night-watchman state", a minimal state only concerned with citizens' primary needs. The power of the state must be unlimited inside the limits proper to each state. From this it follows that the question concerning the form of the state becomes a secondary one. Most important, instead, is the basic conception of the state in general, i.e. of the lawful organization of the state. In addition to this, Schelling emphasizes that the state is by no means useless or worthless. It is something that is negative, but it is oriented towards the positive.

II

This very brief account of Schelling's conception of the state makes it quite clear that Schelling does not want to get involved with the specific problems implied by Hegel's theory of the state. Schelling's own account remains aphoristic, and he does not explain directly why it is necessary to limit the functions of the state. The explanation emerges only later, when he attempts to formulate his own view of the transcendental meaning of history. Alexander Hollerbach has pointed out that this formulation, too, is aimed against Hegel's philosophy. I shall therefore briefly comment on it.

Schelling argues that Hegel – like so many others – does not understand that the dissolving relationships, which formerly held human life together, are merely *real* relationships. They are not *ideal* or freedom-based relationships. Human communities and unities are in fact annihilated to mere atoms to make room for a higher, ideal unity. Humanity cannot exist without unity, and when one unity is annihilated, this is to be seen merely as a sign of a new and higher unity. The highly popular individualistic attempts to dissolve the state into smaller states and movements are incapable of considering those winds of change that necessarily follow in the wake of the birth of a higher spirit. To this spirit the state and all its apparatuses only represent the "raw-material" that it uses in building a world according to its own ends. The new spirit builds a world which lasts forever and cannot be annihilated. This ideal (but real!) world has nothing to do with the servility which is so pervasive in all the attempts to ground the world in the state. Schelling maintains that if you are interested in freedom, you ought not to concentrate all your efforts on developing a strong state-power (because it can never be strong enough). Instead, you ought to limit the power of the state.

Schelling says that the state is an order of transition. Its function is purely transitional. The state is a means by which real unity can be established and guaranteed between humans. The state is not an end in itself. It can only serve us if we try to build and realize the highest possible end, in other words, ideal unity. It is important to notice here that earlier Schelling himself had thought that the state is the highest possible end. But formulations such as "setting the state above everything" are, of course, directed against Hegel. Hegel failed because he misunderstood the real order of things, which originates from God. "The real home of humans is in the heaven, in other words, in the world of ideas. The humans must return to their real home and find their place from there". The attainment of this goal presupposes an about-turn (*Umkehrung*) which will lead to a new order of things. It will lead to an order where "justice dwells and has staying-power, which means the real and true relation".

It can be seen from this that the social thought of Schelling is oriented towards a transcendental and eschatological goal, including its realization. It may be asked, however, whence this end or goal finds its ground and measure. In this context it is interesting to note that Schelling emphasizes the role of "justice" (*Gerechtigkeit*) in the attainment of the goal. Here the order of justice means the just and true relation. But this "rechte und wahre Verhältnis" is understood as an objective order in which justice and truth belong together. Justice is the highest world-law (*Weltgesetz*). It grants everyone their rights and guarantees everyone their own sphere of action. "Every voice, those of the Greek poets included, testifies to what Hebrew poets have said of the God in their own way: Justice (*Gerechtigkeit*) and Court (*Gericht*) are His throne". It must be admitted that Schelling does not say this in direct connection with the sphere of the social. What he does say, however, is relevant to social philosophy because of the universal reference of his statement. Justice means *suum cuique*, i.e. being just towards everyone in his/her own sphere and in his/her own relationship. This is the highest law. It is an essential feature of God, says Schelling, referring explicitly to Psalms 89,15 and 97,2. This means that there is no absolute justice.

I wish to thank my sister Kaisa Sivenius for her help in revising my English.

References

Sources

Hegel, G. W. F. 1942. *The Philosophy of Right*. Oxford: At the Clarendon Press. Translated by T. M. Knox. (1821)

Schelling, F. 1856-61. *Friedrich Wilhelm Joseph von Schellings sämmtliche Werke*. Edited by Karl Friedrich A. Schelling. 14. vols. Stuttgart/Augsburg: J. G. Cotta'scher Verlag.

Schelling, F. *Grundlegung der positiven Philosophie*. Münchner Vorlesung. Wintersemester 1832/33 and Sommersemester 1833. Turin, Bottega d'Erasmo, 1972. Edited by Horst Fuhrmans. (Philosophica varia inedita vel rariora.)

Schelling, F. 1833/34. *Geschichte der philosophischen Systeme von Cartesius bis auf die gegenwärtige Zeit als Übergang zum System der positiven Philosophie*. Münchener Vorlesungen. Wintersemester 1833/34.

Literature

Beach, E. A. 1994. *The potencies of God(s). Schelling's philosophy of mythology*. Albany: State University of New York Press.

Frauenstädt, J. 1842. *Schellings Vorlesungen in Berlin. Darstellung und Kritik der Hauptpunkte derselben mit besonderer Beziehung auf das Verhältnis zwischen Christentum und Philosophie*. Berlin.

Fuhrmans, H. 1955/56. Dokumente zur Schellingforschung. *Kant-Studien.* Bd. 47, 182-191, 273-287, 378-396.

Fuhrmans, H. 1956. Schelling-Briefe aus Anlass seiner Berufung nach München im Jahre 1827. *Philosophisches Jahrbuch der Görres-Gesellschaft.* 64 Jahrgang, 272-297. (Fuhrmans 1956a)

Fuhrmans, H. 1956/57. Der Ausgangspunkt der Schellingschen Spätphilosophie. Dokumente zur Schellingforschung. *Kant-Studien.* Bd. 48, 302-323. (Fuhrmans 1956b)

Habermas, J. 1954. *Das Absolute und die Geschichte. Von der Zwiespältigkeit in Schellings Denken.* Inaugural-Dissertation zur Erlangung der Doktorwürde der Philosophischen Fakultät der Universität Bonn. Bonn: Bouvier. (Abhandlungen zur Philosophie, Psychologie und Pädagogik, Bd. 1.)

Hollerbach, A. 1957. *Der Rechtsgedanke bei Schelling. Quellenstudien zu seiner Rechts- und Staatsphilosophie.* Frankfurt am Main: Vittorio Klostermann. (Philosophische Abhandlungen, Bd. 13.)

Schulz, W. 1954. Das Verhältnis des späten Schelling zu Hegel. Schellings Spekulation über den Satz. *Zeitschrift für Philosophische Forschung.* Bd. 8, 336-352.

Other SoPhi Publications in English

Mirja Satka

Making Social Citizenship
Conceptual Practices from the Finnish Poor Law to professional social work

"This is an impressive, important, and original piece of work. It contributes to a growing body of studies of 'the relations of ruling' and of the significance of texts and concepts in the social organization of professional work, particularly social work. In general this approach avoids the traditional split between theory and practice, ideas and action... Treatment of texts and textuality as features of organization transforms the traditional history of ideas."
Dorothy E. Smith, Professor of Sociology, University of Toronto

"Substantively, author's ability to construct and deconstruct historical data and to link social welfare development to the emergent of the modern state, supported by detailed argument and supporting data, is exceptional."
Stephen M. Rose, Professor of Social Welfare,
University of New England

Mirja Satka's study provides an adept and original analysis of developing conceptual practices in the social welfare field. She writes a different history of ideas in the context of the state formation of a small country. Satka analyzes the conceptual innovations of the discursive pioneers in the social relations of class and gender and interprets them as organizing practices in the developing relations of ruling. The study provides a socially extended understanding of both the role and discourse of poor relief and social work.

Mirja Satka is Senior Lecturer of Social Work at the University of Jyväsky-lä, Finland.

SoPhi 1, 1996 (2nd edition), ISBN 951-34-0642-3, price FIM 106

Tuija Parvikko & Jukka Kanerva (eds.)

Exploring the Chronospace of Images

The desire to master the entire globe - or at least known parts of it - is as old as human civilization. Formerly, the pursuit often appeared as intentional and deliberate control over human action and life-conducts, mostly in concrete manners. In the contemporary world, however, the public and private are no longer simple physical spheres, but rather image spaces created in the visual spaces like photography, television and internet. The ancient human desire to control these spheres takes such forms as Luciano Benetton's ecumenical fantasy to overcome cultural differences and to master the entire globe. This book attempts to find new ways of tackling the public and private bringing together the textual and visual ways of approaching them. It seeks for new spaces for intellectual exchange in order to overcome the hierarchical distinction between center and periphery.

Introduction
I The Conquest of the Orbis Terrarum in the Chronospace of Images
Michael Shapiro: Images of Planetary Danger. Luciano Benetton's Ecumenical Fantasy
Jukka Kanerva: Oikoumenon and Benetton's Images
Ari Turunen: Centers and Peripheries. The Construction of Ecumenical Space on World Maps
II The Rhetoric of Images
Kimmo Lehtonen: On the Relationship between Visuality and Rhetoric
Juha Virkki: Sociality in the Age of Mediascape. The Uses of Media, Control of Distance, and Social Agency
III Private and Public in Religious Life-conduct
Marjo Kaartinen: Humanism Colliding with Humanism. Public and Private Spheres in the English Religious Debate on Monasticism from c. 1510 to 1540
Kari Palonen: How to Turn God into an Ally? The Rhetoric of Life-conduct in Max Weber's 'Protestant Ethic'
IV Image-Space of Political Action
Kia Lindroos: The Shopping Bag Lady and Politics. Visualization and Temporalization of Politics through Benjaminian Ideas
Tuija Parvikko: The Pariah as a Rebel. From Identity Politics to the Politics of Rootlessness

SoPhi 4, ISBN 951-34-0744-6, price FIM 100

Tuija Parvikko

The Responsibility of the Pariah

"Tuija Parvikko adds significantly to the (often controversial) understanding of Hannah Arendt and deals at the same time with the question of political and personal responsibility, different forms and situations of the socially and politically excluded pariah, anti-Semitism, the destruction of European Jewry, the supposed innocence of victims, genocide, xenophobia, and other questions of the utmost historical as well as current political significance. Tuija Parvikko's book is an exciting journey through a lot of important issues in historical and contemporary politics and the notion of the political."
Dr. Klaus Sondermann, University of Tampere.

Winner of the Doctoral Thesis Award of the Finnish Science Academy 1997.

Tuija Parvikko's study deals with the textual archeology and history of Hannah Arendt's conception of pariahdom. It shows that Arendt's impact on political theory is not restricted to the theorization of political action in the public realm under "normal" circumstances but that her considerations of pariahdom constitute an important source for theorizing the political in extreme situations.

Tuija Parvikko is Assistant Professor of Political Science at the University of Jyväskylä, Finland.

SoPhi 7, ISBN 951-34-0795-0, price FIM 100

Finnish Yearbook of
Political Thought 1997 vol. 1

Finland has been a country with several competing intellectual centres regarding the reception and formulation of political thought. The ideas of Scandinavian, German, French, Anglo-American and Russian political thought have all been present in the Finnishn intellectual arena. However, their international confrontations as well their Finnish receptions and mixtures are still poorly represented in Finland and abroad. *Finnish Yearbook of Political Thought* is a response to these considerations.

The first volume concentrates on Reinhart Koselleck's conceptual history. It is published in collaboration with The Finnish Political Science Association and The Finnish Historical Society.

Introduction. Reflections on Political Thought in Finland
Reinhart Koselleck: Temporalisation of Concepts
Melvin Richter: Appreciating A Contemporary Classic. The *Geschihctliche Grundbegriffe* and Future Scholarship
Kari Palonen: An Application of Conceptual History to Itself. From Method to Theory in Reinhart Koselleck's *Begriffsgeschichte*
Sisko Haikala: Criticism in the Enlightenment. Prespectives to Koselleck's *Kritik und Krise* Study
Tuija Pulkkinen: The Postmodern Moment of Political Theory
Eerik Lagerspetz: The Philosophy of Democracy and the Paradoxes of Majority Rule
Book Reviews

SoPhi 10, ISBN 951-34-0926-0, price FIM 70

Send orders to

Kampus Kirja
Kauppakatu 9, FIN-40100 Jyväskylä, Finland
tel.+358-(0)14-603157, fax +358-(0)14-611143
e-mail kkirja@bibelot.jyu.fi

Pay by VISA, or Eurocard, or as per invoice upon receipt of the books. If paying by credit card state your name, address and card expiration date. Please sign your order.

SoPhi books are also sold by quality bookshops.

Visit our WWW-page at http://www.jyu.fi/~yhtfil/sop2.html